Robert Feinschreiber is a graduate of Yale Law School and received his M.B.A. in accounting and finance from Columbia University. He also holds an LLM in taxation from New York University and a B.A. from Trinity College.

Mr. Feinschreiber is presently an attorney in private practice in New York City. Prior to that he was associated with a national CPA firm and was the assistant chief accountant for Joseph E. Seagram and Sons. In the past, he was an assistant professor of law at Wayne State University and taught accounting at Yale University. He served the Chrysler Corporation as Federal Income Tax Supervisor, and was the Director of Taxation and Financial Analysis for the National Association of Manufacturers. Mr. Feinschreiber is a director of the International Tax Institute, and is a member of the American Bar Association (Tax Section Committee on Depreciation and Amortization), The New York State Bar Association, The Association of the Bar of The City of New York, New York County Lawyers Association, and The Tax Society of New York University.

He has written numerous articles for such publications as *The CPA Journal, Journal of Taxation, The Tax Adviser, Taxation for Accountants,* and *Taxes—The Tax Magazine,* and is the editor of the *International Tax Journal.*

Tax Depreciation
under the
Class Life
ADR System

Robert Feinschreiber

Tax Depreciation
under the
Class Life
ADR System

amacom
A division of American Management Associations

Library of Congress Cataloging in Publication Data

Feinschreiber, Robert.
    Tax depreciation under the Class Life ADR System.

    Includes bibliographical references and index.
    1. Class Life ADR system. 2. Depreciation
allowances--United States. I. Title.
HJ465.3.D5F44   343'.73'068   75-4583
ISBN 0-8144-5397-X

First Printing

To my Mother, Maxine Feinschreiber,
whose love and encouragement have proved
to be an important inspiration.

Contents

Tax Depreciation
under the
Class Life
ADR System

1

General Aspects

1.1 Introduction

This book is designed as a practical guide to one of the most important tax deductions available to a business, Class Life ADR depreciation. Thus, it is written for financial executives, accountants, attorneys, tax managers and staff, and others involved in tax depreciation planning or compliance. The importance of tax depreciation derives not only from the sheer magnitude of the deductions but from its many discretionary aspects. Because a business can use tax depreciation to substantially alter its tax liability, full knowledge of the depreciation rules together with careful planning can yield substantial benefits.

Class Life ADR depreciation is complex, but the book provides a comprehensive explanation of its provisions with the goal of enabling taxpayers to use this new depreciation system to best advantage. Toward that end, the book compares Class Life ADR depreciation with conventional depreciation and emphasizes the aspects of greatest present and future practical benefit.

During 1971, the Internal Revenue Service initiated the Asset Depreciation Range (ADR) System to liberalize tax depreciation for assets placed in service in 1971 or thereafter.* This new depreciation system was attacked as lacking in statutory authority, but specific legislation was forthcoming later that year.† This depreciation sys-

*Feinschreiber, "Depreciation Reform: Recent Treasury Study Reveals Liberalization Alternatives," *Journal of Taxation,* October 1970, p. 204; Feinschreiber, "New Regulations Liberalize Tax Depreciation," *The New York Certified Public Accountant,* September 1971, p. 637.

†Feinschreiber, "Revenue Act of 1971 Contains Many Little Noticed but Far Reaching Provisions," *Taxation for Accountants,* January 1972, p. 4.

1

tem, as revised by statute, is officially called the Class Life Asset Depreciation Range System. Some commentators refer to this new group of rules as "ADR," while others use the term "Class Life." To avoid confusion with the Guideline Class Life rules for assets acquired and placed in service before 1971, this book uses the term "Class Life ADR" for the above-described depreciation system.

The Class Life ADR depreciation system is optional for each taxpayer. Taxpayers that do not elect the Class Life ADR System must base their depreciation deductions on "facts and circumstances." Where appropriate, references to facts-and-circumstances depreciation and the Guideline Class Life System are made.

To simplify the footnotes, all references to Regulations issued under Section 1.167(a) are referred to solely by the part of the citation following the dash. For example, Sec. 1.167(a)–11(d)(3)(vii)(d)(2) is identified as 11(d)(3)(vii)(d)(2).

The principal advantage of the Class Life ADR System is that it provides, for most assets, a 20 percent reduction in asset useful life, and thus accelerates depreciation deductions. The system is designed to minimize disputes between taxpayers and the Internal Revenue Service as to useful life, salvage value, repairs, and other matters.[1] This goal is substantially realized as to useful life, but not for the other objectives.*

Election of the Class Life ADR System encompasses all eligible assets unless an optional exclusion applies.[2] Included assets must remain in the Class Life ADR System in later years.[3] However, the Class Life ADR System need not be elected for assets placed in service in a later year, even if elected for a prior year.[4]

In general, a taxpayer must establish accounts by year of acquisition and asset classification (vintage accounts), must select a depreciation period (useful life) and compute the depreciation deduction, and must apply rules pertaining to averaging conventions, salvage value, retirements, and repairs.[5] A taxpayer cannot elect to apply some, but less than all, Class Life ADR rules except that the repair rules need not be adopted.[6] Taxpayers electing to use the Class Life ADR depreciation system must also comply with detailed reporting requirements.[7] Regulations provide that depreciation computed under Class Life ADR will constitute a reasonable allowance for depreciation under the tax law.[8]

---

[1]Numbered references pertain to official source citations and appear at the end of each chapter.
*Feinschreiber, "How and When to Use Class Life Depreciation." *Prentice-Hall Tax Ideas,* July 18, 1973, paragraph 15,020.

1.2 Vintage Accounts

If the Class Life ADR depreciation system is utilized, all included assets must be grouped into special types of accounts called "vintage accounts."[9] Vintage accounts are "closed end" accounts.[10] Thus, a vintage account includes assets placed in service only during a particular taxable year. Assets placed in service in an earlier or later taxable year, even if identical, are placed in different vintage accounts. The "vintage" of an account refers to the taxable year during which the property in the account is first placed in service by the taxpayer.[11]

A vintage account must include assets from only one guideline class.[12] Eligible assets are divided into approximately 120 guideline classes. These classes can be divided into the following categories (references are to the official asset guideline class numbers):[13]

1. Transportation equipment (such as trucks, airplanes, automobiles), 00.21–00.28.
2. Specific industries, 01.1–50.0, 79.0.
3. Buildings and land improvements, 00.3, 65.11–65.43.
4. Office furniture and equipment, 70.11–70.13.
5. Miscellaneous, 70.2.

Most taxpayers, unless they are highly diversified, will find that their industrial equipment comes within a small number of asset guideline classes.

Assets must be included in the asset guideline class for the activity in which the property is primarily used.[14] Property is classified according to primary use, even though the activity in which the property is primarily used is insubstantial in relation to the taxpayer's activities.[15] This latter rule is a change from the Guideline depreciation system in effect from 1962 to 1970. See *Section 1.4** concerning the reclassification of property.

A vintage account may consist of a single asset or a group of assets within a guideline class.[16] Any number of vintage accounts may be established for a guideline class.[17] Thus, more than one account of the same vintage may be established for different assets of the same guideline class.[18] However, it will be advantageous in almost all situations to use as few vintage accounts as possible and place as many assets as possible in the same vintage accounts. This result occurs because vintage accounts are grouped together to deny deduc-

---

*References to numbered sections in this book are shown in italic type as "*Section.*" References to portions of official documents are shown in roman type as "Section."

tions for losses on retirements, whereas they are treated separately when gain is recognized.[19]

In certain situations, the Regulations mandate that more than one vintage account be used, even though the assets are in the same guideline class and are acquired during the same taxable year. These situations are described in the subsequent paragraphs.

Section 1245 property may not be placed in the same vintage account as Section 1250 property.[20] This particular rule is of limited impact because Section 1245 property and Section 1250 property are usually not within the same guideline class. However, if the primary use of an asset changes so that it becomes Section 1250 instead of Section 1245 property, no change in vintage account classification is made.[21]

Property eligible for the reduction in salvage value by up to 10 percent of the basis of the asset may not be placed in a vintage account with ineligible property.[22] Generally, personal property (except livestock) with a useful life of 3 years or more is eligible, so that it is rare to find both eligible and ineligible assets in the same guideline class. Consequently, this rule has little applicability.

The tax law also provides limited amounts of additional first-year depreciation.[23] The Regulations provide that assets eligible for and utilizing the additional first-year depreciation may not be grouped with ineligible assets or eligible assets for which additional first-year depreciation is not elected.[24] This rule is of limited applicability because additional first-year depreciation is minor for most companies.

The requirement of a separate vintage account for property receiving additional first-year depreciation has one confusing aspect: For purposes of the Class Life ADR System, the unadjusted basis is asset cost less additional first-year depreciation.[25] Thus, the reason for requiring separate vintage accounts for such assets is unclear.

In determining the particular vintage of an asset, the criterion is the date placed in service.[26] The actual date is to be used, so this determination is independent of the first-year averaging convention selected by the taxpayer.[27]

1.3 Depreciation Ranges and Periods

Each vintage account (as defined in *Section 1.2*) and each guideline class has an "asset guideline period."[28] For some guideline classes, such as buildings and land improvements, the asset guideline period is the mandatory useful life.[29] For most asset guideline classes, the asset depreciation period is not the only permissible useful life.[30] Instead, the asset depreciation period is the midpoint of the "asset depreciation range," which is the range of useful lives for a vintage account.[31]

The asset depreciation range for a guideline class extends from 80 percent of the asset guideline period to 120 percent of the asset guideline period.[32] In other words, the useful life can be increased or decreased by 20 percent from the asset guideline period. For example, if the asset guideline period is 10 years, then a taxpayer may use a useful life as short as 8 years or as long as 12 years. Normally, the shortest life will be selected, provided the investment credit is not reduced.

Generally, the asset depreciation period may be any whole number of years or any whole number plus a half-year within the asset depreciation range,[33] so that in the case of an asset with a guideline period of 10 years, the permissible lives are 8, 8.5, 9, 9.5, 10, 10.5, 11, 11.5, and 12. Where the 20 percent increase or 20 percent decrease in useful life does not result in a whole number or a whole number plus a half-year, the maximum and minimum of the range must be rounded to the nearest half or whole year. Thus, if the guideline period is 7 years, a 20 percent reduction would yield a life of 5.6. Rounding to the nearest half-year, the minimum life is 5.5.

In general, the shorter the asset life, the better for the taxpayer, but there are three basic exceptions to this general rule:

1. A taxpayer with net operating losses or a low effective tax rate may find it advantageous to use longer asset lives. Such a taxpayer may likely find it preferable to lease rather than purchase the assets.

2. Use of a short asset life may cause a reduction in the investment credit, as the following table indicates.*

Life (Years)	Investment Credit
Under 3	0
3 or longer, but less than 5	$\frac{1}{3} \times 7\%$
5 or longer, but less than 7	$\frac{2}{3} \times 7\%$
7 or longer	$\frac{3}{3} \times 7\%$

The same life as used for depreciation purposes must be used for the investment credit.[34]

3. Accelerated depreciation is generally not available when an asset has a life of less than 3 years.

Table 1 is intended to provide some general guidance as to useful life selection, taking into account the second and third factors men-

*Feinschreiber, "How to Maximize Tax Savings Under the Revived Investment Credit," *Prentice-Hall Tax Ideas,* ¶ 15,026.

TABLE 1

Asset Guideline Period	Permissible Lives	Best Alternative(s)
3	2.5,3,3.5	3
4	3,3.5,4,4.5,5	3,5
5	4,4.5,5,5.5,6	4,5
6	5,5.5,6,6.5,7	5,7
7	5.5,6,6.5,7,7.5,8,8.5	5.5,7
8	6.5,7,7.5,8,8.5,9,9.5	6.5,7
> 8		As short as possible

tioned above. These results are generalizations, and each taxpayer should make its own determinations.

Asset guideline classes, periods, and depreciation ranges were initially established by Revenue Procedure 72-10.[35] New classes, periods, and ranges may be established by the Internal Revenue Service.[36] Some such amendments have already been made.[37]

Retroactivity of these revisions is limited. Taxpayers may generally use the lives in effect at either the beginning or the end of the taxable year.[38] Changes made after the close of the taxable year are not retroactive, even if favorable, unless specifically provided.[39]

1.4 Asset Classification

As indicated in *Section 1.2,* property is to be classified according to its primary use, even if that activity is insubstantial in relation to the taxpayer's other activities.[40]

If an asset is incorrectly categorized by a taxpayer, or erroneously treated as ineligible, the classification of the property must be corrected.[41] Neither the taxpayer nor the Internal Revenue Service may terminate the Class Life ADR election as the result of this misclassification.[42] The Regulations provide specific procedures for making these corrections.

As part of the correction process, all adjustments necessary for the correction must be made, including (where necessary) unadjusted basis, adjusted basis, salvage value, and depreciation reserve of all affected vintage accounts.[43] Depreciation deductions also must be adjusted for all open years.[44]

If an asset was erroneously excluded from the Class Life ADR System, the taxpayer must place the property in a vintage account and select an appropriate asset depreciation period as part of the adjustment process.[45] If an asset was included, but the depreciation period was selected from the wrong asset depreciation range, that error must also be corrected.[46]

Some taxpayers can exclude certain asset categories* from the Class Life ADR System when the depreciation method is not based on years for at least 75 percent of the assets in that category.[47] Where misclassfications of assets erroneously cause this test to be met, these methods may no longer be used.[48] If the taxpayer establishes that the mistake was made in good faith, the change will be prospective only.[49]

1.5 Collateral Effects

In general, the useful life selected for Class Life ADR purposes is binding for all purposes of the tax law. Thus, the election constitutes a binding agreement under Section 167(d) as to useful life.[50] The election also terminates any prior Section 167(d) agreements (which were rarely used) as to property eligible for the Class Life ADR System, but does not affect other property covered by the agreement.[51]

Thus, the useful life selected for purposes of the Class Life ADR System must be utilized for the following purposes:[52]

1. Investment credit[53] (see *Section 1.3*).
2. The tax on tax preferences.[54]
3. The computation of investment expenses for purposes of the limitation on the deductibility of investment interest.[55]
4. The requirement that an asset have a useful life of at least 3 years for acceleration depreciation to apply.[56]
5. The requirement that an asset have at least a 3-year life for the salvage value reduction of up to 10 percent of basis to apply.[57]
6. The requirement that an asset have a useful life of at least 6 years to obtain additional first-year depreciation.[58]
7. Depreciation for earnings and profits purposes.[59]
8. The tax imposed on tax-exempt organizations with respect to debt-financed income.[60]
9. The excise tax imposed on private foundations.[61]

For three purposes, the life selected under the Class Life ADR System is not determinative.

1. Salvage value, the residual value at the end of an asset's useful life, must be determined for all assets. For purposes of this determination, actual useful life—not the Class Life—is to be utilized.[62] This rule is an important facet of the Class Life ADR System because

*See *Section 2.6* at p. 20.

estimated salvage value is normally much lower at the end of actual useful life than at the end of the asset depreciation period.

2. One factor in determining whether an expenditure is a deductible repair or a capitalized item is whether the expenditure prolongs the life of the asset. For purposes of this determination, actual useful life—not the Class Life—is to be utilized.[63]

3. One factor that determines whether a transaction constitutes a sale or lease is the useful life of the property that is the subject of the transaction. For purposes of this determination, actual life—not Class Life—is to be utilized.[64]

In these instances in which the Class Life is not utilized, each taxpayer is faced with the necessity (and opportunity) of determining the actual useful life for each asset.

For certain purposes within the tax law, straight-line depreciation must be computed even though accelerated depreciation is otherwise utilized for an asset or an account. In such a situation, the same life that is otherwise utilized must also be employed for purposes of the straight-line depreciation computation.[65]

1.6 Basis

The general rules for asset basis, apart from the Class Life ADR System, specify that basis for depreciation purposes is the adjusted basis for determining gain on the sale or other disposition of the asset.[66]

The Class Life ADR System contains more detailed rules that differentiate between adjusted basis and unadjusted basis. The unadjusted basis of an asset is its cost or other basis, without any adjustment for depreciation or amortization, other than additional first-year depreciation.[67]

This rule also applies to excluded additions (capitalized expenditures ineligible for the repair allowance)[68] and to property improvements (expenditures eligible for the repair allowance but above the repair allowance ceiling).[69] Thus, the unadjusted basis of a "special basis vintage account" is the amount of property improvements in the account.[70]

The unadjusted basis of a vintage account is the total of the unadjusted bases of all assets in the account.[71]

The adjusted basis of a vintage account is the amount by which the unadjusted basis of the account exceeds the depreciation reserve for the account.[72] Similarly, the adjusted basis of an asset in a vintage account is the unadjusted basis minus depreciation.[73] Depreciation for the asset is computed using the method of depreciation and the rate applicable to the account.[74]

When a portion of an asset is retired, the depreciation attributable to the asset (in that situation only) includes the amount of proceeds previously added to the reserve upon the retirement of portions of the asset.[75]

1.7 Election

The Class Life ADR System is elective with each taxpayer.[76] The election is annual, so that an election in one taxable year binds all assets placed in service during that year, but does not have any effect on assets placed in service in a following taxable year.[77]

A taxpayer's election of the Class Life ADR System may not be revoked or modified after the last day prescribed for filing the election, except for taxable years beginning before 1973.[78]

In general, the Class Life ADR System is elected on the tax return filed for the year that the property was placed in service.[79] If the taxpayer does not file a timely return, taking extensions into account, the election is made at the time the return is ultimately filed.[80]

The Class Life ADR election cannot be made on an amended return. However, for prior taxable years, the election could be made on an amended return if filed by the later of the times prescribed for filing the return, including extensions, or September 20, 1973.[81] If an election is not made in a timely manner, no election may be made for assets placed in service during that taxable year, whether by amended return or otherwise.[82]

In the case of affiliated corporations[83] filing a consolidated return, each corporation may or may not elect the Class Life ADR System.[84] This provision is important for tax planning. In some situations in which it is desired to include some eligible assets while excluding others, this goal may be obtainable through the use of multiple corporations.

Where property is placed in service by a trust, estate, or partnership, the election is made by the entity, not by the beneficiary or the partner.[85] Thus, if the entity does not make the election, the Class Life ADR System will not apply to the beneficiaries or to the partners.[86]

Some special election rules applied during the early years of the Class Life ADR System. For taxable years beginning before 1973, a taxpayer could make, amend, or revoke the Class Life ADR election within 150 days after the last of three events:[87] (1) the time the first tax return is filed by the taxpayer for that year,[88] (2) April 23, 1973,[89] or (3) the time prescribed by law, including extensions, for filing the tax return.[90]

If the election was filed within a specified time period, it will be regarded as valid if it conforms to Class Life ADR rules and was not amended or revoked by the taxpayer.[91] An election that did not conform to these rules had to be amended or the Class Life ADR System would not apply.[92]

Presently, the election can be made only in accordance with Form 4832.[93] Errors in compliance will not normally terminate the election. The election will not be rendered invalid so long as there is substantial compliance, in good faith, with the information requirements.[94] The election requires that ten items of information be supplied:

1. The election must state that the taxpayer does make the election and consents to (and agrees to apply) all provisions in the Class Life ADR System.[95]

2. The election must specify the asset guideline class for each vintage account placed in service during the taxable year.[96]

3. The election must specify the useful life (asset depreciation period) for each vintage account,[97] which must be either a whole year or a whole year plus a half-year.[98]

4. The election must specify the first-year averaging convention utilized.[99] Only the half-year convention and the modified half-year convention are permissible.[100] If the modified half-year convention is utilized, the basis of property placed in service must be indicated for each half-year.[101] Form 4832 requires the information on a half-year basis regardless of the averaging convention elected.

5. The unadjusted basis, salvage value, and salvage value reduction of up to 10-percent basis where applicable,[102] must be indicated for each vintage account.[103] Note that gross salvage value rather than net salvage value must be utilized.[104]

6. The election must indicate whether used property is excluded.[105]

7. For each guideline class for which the repair allowance is elected, the election must state the amount of capitalized repairs, called "property improvements."[106] The election must also indicate whether the amount of property improvements, called a "special basis vintage account," is allocated to retirements.[107]

8. The election must indicate whether any assets were excluded under any of the following provisions:[108] property subject to rapid amortization,[109] property depreciation under a method not based on years,[110] buildings placed in service before 1974,[111] subsidiary

assets,[112] utility property for which the deferral is not normalized,[113] pre–1971 property acquired from an affiliate,[114] and a limited category of investment credit property transferred between affiliates.[115] The taxpayer must maintain a reasonable description of the excluded property and the justification for the exclusion.[116]

9. The election must also indicate whether any assets eligible for the pre-repeal investment credit are excluded.[117] Data on the assets must be maintained by the taxpayer, including description and justification for exclusion.[118]

10. The election must also include other required information, such as data concerning a composite guideline class for a gas utility.[119]

Certain additional information is required for asset retirements: unadjusted basis, proceeds, and vintage (year placed in service).[120] All accounts of the same vintage and asset guideline class may be treated as a single account for purposes of this rule.[121] Books and records must be maintained to substantiate this data.[122] A transfer of an asset to supplies or scrap as a means of retirement does not necessitate this full reporting.[123]

Additional repair allowance data is also required if the repair allowance is elected. This data includes information about repairs, maintenance, rehabilitation, and improvement of assets.[124]

If mass assets are utilized, the taxpayer must indicate whether a standard mortality dispersion curve is used or whether the curve is based upon the taxpayer's own experience.[125] Other information may also be required.[126] The cross-reference provided in the Regulations is incorrect. It should read (d)(3)(v)(d)(1), not (d)(3)(v)(c).

1.8 Miscellaneous Provisions

A few provisions within the Class Life ADR System are of limited applicability or are difficult to categorize. These provisions are discussed in this section.

1.8.1 Composite Guideline Classes—Utilities

Electric and gas utilities were given limited permission under Rev. Proc. 64-21 to use a composite guideline class. These taxpayers, and only these taxpayers, may use a composite guideline class within the Class Life ADR System.[127]

The composite asset guideline period in effect at the time the Class Life ADR System is first elected is to be used initially.[128] The asset depreciation range is to be based on that asset depreciation period.[129] The asset depreciation range and period are not changed until major variations in the asset mix or asset guideline classes or periods justify some other composite asset guideline period.[130] All property in the composite asset guideline class, except buildings and other structures, is treated as though included in a single asset guideline class.[131]

If an electric or gas utility elects to use a composite guideline class, the election must be made for the first taxable year in which the Class Life ADR System is utilized. The elected guideline class is binding on future years in which the Class Life ADR System is elected, unless the Internal Revenue Service grants permission to terminate the use of a composite guideline class.[132] Presumably, the change must be requested on Form 3115.

1.8.2 Normalization for Public Utility Property

In many situations, public utilities are required to "normalize" their tax depreciation, a term to be examined below. If normalization is required, public utility property is eligible for the Class Life ADR System only if the tax deferral resulting from that system is normalized.[133]

A utility will be considered to have normalized the tax deferral generated by the Class Life ADR System only if (1) "tax expense" used for rate-making purposes and reflecting operations is based on a depreciation period no shorter than the asset guideline period or the depreciation period used for rate-making purposes, whichever is shorter; and (2) makes an adjustment to the reserve for taxes.[134]

The following example illustrates the normalization of the tax deferral resulting from the use of the Class Life ADR depreciation system.[135] Here, DDB and SL represent "double declining balance" and "straight line," respectively.

	CL/ADR	Rate-Making	Difference
Unadjusted basis, $	2,000,000	2,000,000	
Life, years	17.5	22	
Method	DDB	SL	
Convention	Half-year	Half-year	
Depreciation (first year), $	114,285	45,454	68,831
Tax rate (percent)			48
Amount added to reserve, $			33,039

The Regulations also contain specific provisions for the determination of useful life where no guideline life had been established by Rev. Proc. 62-21 or where lives were to be established by regulatory agencies. In that situation, the depreciation period used for rate-making purposes, not the Class Life ADR asset guideline period, is to be utilized to determine if normalization has taken place.[136]

If a taxpayer is required to normalize the tax deferral, but fails to do so for any assets, the Class Life ADR election terminates with respect to those assets as of the beginning of the taxable year for which the taxpayer failed to normalize the deferral.[137] This rule will not cause termination of the Class Life ADR System for such assets with respect to a prior taxable year.[138] The depreciation reserve for the account is reduced by the reserve attributable to the assets removed,[139] and salvage value of the account may be reduced by the salvage value attributable to the retired asset.[140]

1.8.3 Property Used Outside the United States

Property used outside the United States may be eligible for the Class Life ADR System if the assets are otherwise eligible.[141] However, the asset depreciation range does not apply to these assets,[142] so useful life may not be shortened by 20 percent. The asset depreciation period and status of the asset as used in the United States or used outside the United States are determined in the taxable year of election and are not modifiable because of a change, after the close of the taxable year of election, in predominant use.[143]

Property used outside the United States will not be considered as placed within the same guideline class as property used within the United States.[144] Instead, a mirror-image set of guideline classes is deemed to exist for property located outside the United States.[145] This rule establishing separate guideline classes does not apply to the repair allowance.[146]

The determination whether property is used inside or outside the United States is generally based on predominant use.[147] However, there are special rules, initially established for investment credit purposes, that determine place of use in many circumstances.[148]

1.8.4 Leased Property

The asset depreciation range and the asset depreciation period of leased assets are independent of the lease term and renewal periods[149] unless the asset is excluded as leasehold improvement and is amortized.[150] Unless a separate asset guideline class has been established for lessors (and such classes have not yet been established), the asset guideline class for the property is determined as if the property is owned by the lessee.[151] Where the asset guideline class is based upon the type of property (such as trucks or railroad cars), rather than on the activity in which the asset is used, the property classification is independent of the use of the asset by the lessee.[152] However, a different rule applies in limited situations to leases or binding contracts entered into between March 13, 1971, and April 22, 1973.[153]

1.8.5 New Taxpayers

A new taxpayer will normally have a taxable year of less than 12 full calendar months. Even under the Class Life ADR System, depreciation is allowed only for the actual number of months.[154] The Class Life ADR System contains rules for dividing such a taxable year so as to apply the modified half-year convention.[155]

REFERENCES

1. 11(a)(1).
2. 11(a)(1), 11(b)(5)(ii).
3. 11(a)(1).
4. 11(a)(1).
5. 11(a)(1).
6. 11(a)(1).
7. 11(a)(1), 11(f)(4).
8. 11(b)(1).
9. 11(b)(3)(i), 11(a)(1).
10. 11(b)(3)(i).
11. 11(b)(3)(i).
12. 11(b)(3)(i), 11(b)(4).
13. Rev. Proc. 72–10, 1972–1 CB 721, as amended.
14. 11(b)(4)(iii)(*b*).
15. 11(b)(4)(iii)(*b*).
16. 11(b)(3)(i).
17. 11(b)(3)(i).
18. 11(b)(3)(i).
19. 11(d)(3)(xi), 11(b)(3)(i).
20. 11(b)(3)(ii).
21. 11(b)(4)(iii)(*b*).
22. 11(b)(3)(ii), Section 167(f).
23. Section 179.
24. 11(b)(3)(ii).
25. T.I.R. 1097, August 12, 1971, 717 CCH 8683.
26. 11(b)(3)(i), 11(c)(2).
27. 11(b)(3)(i).
28. 11(b)(4)(i).
29. 11(b)(4)(i)(*a*).
30. 11(b)(4)(i)(*b*).
31. 11(b)(4)(i).
32. 11(b)(4)(i).
33. 11(b)(4)(i).
34. 11(g)(1)(i).
35. 11(b)(4)(ii).
36. 11(b)(4)(ii).
37. Rev. Proc. 73–2, 1973–4 I.R.B. 22;.
    Rev. Proc. 73–3, 1973–1 CB 698;
    Rev. Proc. 73–23, 1973–40 I.R.B. 10;
    Rev. Proc. 73–24, 1973–40 I.R.B. 11;
    Rev. Proc. 73–25, 1973–40 I.R.B. 13;
    Rev. Proc. 73–26, 1973–40 I.R.B. 14;
    Rev. Proc. 73–28, 1973–40 I.R.B. 17;
    Rev. Proc. 73–30, 1973–42 I.R.B. 17.
38. 11(b)(4)(i).
39. 11(b)(4)(i).
40. 11(b)(4)(iii)(*b*).
41. 11(b)(4)(iii)(*c*).
42. 11(b)(4)(iii)(*c*).
43. 11(b)(4)(iii)(*c*).
44. 11(b)(4)(iii)(*c*).
45. 11(b)(4)(iii)(*c*).
46. 11(b)(4)(iii)(*c*).
47. 11(b)(5)(v)(*a*).
48. 11(b)(4)(iii)(*c*).
49. 11(b)(4)(iii)(*c*).
50. 11(g)(1)(i).
51. 11(g)(2).
52. 11(g)(1)(i).
53. Section 46, Section 47, Section 48.
54. Section 57.
55. Section 163(d)(3)(C).
56. Section 167(c).
57. Section 167(f).

58. Section 179.
59. Section 312(m); Reg. Sec. 1.964–1(c)(1)(iii); Reg. Sec. 1.312–15.
60. Section 514(a)(3).
61. Section 4940(c)(3)(B)(i).
62. 11(g)(1)(ii)(*a*).
63. 11(g)(1)(ii)(*b*).
64. 11(g)(1)(ii)(*c*).
65. 11(g)(3)(1).
66. Reg. Sec. 1.167(g)-1.
67. Section 179, 11(c)(1)(v)(*a*).
68. 11(c)(1)(v)(*a*), 11(d)(2)(vi).
69. 11(c)(1)(v)(*a*), 11(d)(2)(vii).
70. 11(d)(3)(vi), 11(d)(2)(vii)(*a*).
71. 11(c)(1)(v)(*a*).
72. 11(c)(1)(v)(*b*).
73. 11(c)(1)(v)(*b*).
74. 11(c)(1)(v)(*b*).
75. 11(c)(1)(v)(*b*).
76. 11(a)(1).
77. 11(a)(1), 11(b)(5)(i):
78. 11(a)(1)(i), 11(b)(5)(i), 11(f)(1)(iii), 11(f)(3).
79. 11(f)(1)(i).
80. 11(f)(1)(i).
81. 11(f)(1)(i).
82. 11(f)(1)(i).
83. Section 1504(a).
84. 11(f)(1)(i).
85. 11(e)(3)(ii).
86. 11(e)(3)(ii).
87. 11(f)(1)(iii).
88. 11(f)(1)(iii)(*a*).
89. 11(f)(1)(iii)(*b*).
90. 11(f)(1)(iii)(*c*).
91. 11(f)(1)(iii).
92. 11(f)(1)(iii).
93. 11(f)(2).
94. 11(f)(2), 11(f)(4)(ii).
95. 11(f)(2)(i).
96. 11(f)(2)(ii).
97. 11(f)(2)(iii).
98. 11(b)(4)(i).
99. 11(f)(2)(iv).
100. 11(c)(2).
101. 11(f)(2)(iv).
102. Section 167(f).
103. 11(f)(2)(v).
104. 11(d)(1).
105. 11(f)(vi), 11(b)(5)(iii).
106. 11(d)(2)(iii), 11(f)(2)(vii), 11(d)(2)(vii)(*a*).
107. 11(d)(3)(vi), 11(f)(2)(vii).
108. 11(f)(2)(viii).
109. 11(b)(5)(v)(*b*).
110. 11(b)(5)(v)(*a*).
111. 11(b)(5)(vi).
112. 11(b)(5)(vii).
113. 11(b)(6).
114. 11(e)(3)(i).
115. 11(e)(3)(iv).
116. 11(f)(2).
117. 11(f)(ix), 11(b)(5)(iv).
118. 11(f)(2).
119. 11(f)(x), 11(b)(4)(iii)(*a*), 11(f)(4)(ii)(*d*).
120. 11(f)(4)(ii)(*a*), 11(f)(4)(ii)(*b*).
121. 11(f)(4)(ii).
122. 11(f)(4)(i).
123. 11(f)(4)(ii).
124. 11(f)(4)(ii)(*c*).
125. 11(d)(3)(v)(*d*)(*1*), 11(f)(5)(i).
126. 11(f)(5)(ii).
127. 11(b)(4)(iii)(*a*).
128. 11(b)(4)(iii)(*a*)
129. 11(b)(4)(iii)(*a*).
130. 11(b)(4)(iii)(*a*).
131. 11(b)(4)(iii)(*a*).
132. 11(b)(4)(iii)(*a*).
133. 11(b)(6)(i).
134. 11(b)(6)(ii).
135. 11(b)(6)(iv), Example (1).
136. 11(b)(6)(i).
137. 11(b)(6)(iii).
138. 11(b)(6)(iii).
139. 11(b)(6)(iii), 11(c)(1)(v)(*b*).
140. 11(b)(6)(iii), 11(d)(3)(vi)(*c*).
141. Rev. Proc. 72–10, Sec. 2.02.
142. Rev. Proc. 72–10, Sec. 2.02.
143. Rev. Proc. 72–10, Sec. 2.02.
144. Rev. Proc. 72–10, Sec. 2.02.
145. Rev. Proc. 72–10, Sec. 2.02.
146. Rev. Proc. 72–10, Sec. 2.02.
147. Rev. Proc. 72–10, Sec. 2.02.
148. Section 48(a)(2).
149. 11(e)(3)(iii).
150. 11(b)(5)(v), Reg. Sec. 1.162–11(b).
151. 11(e)(3)(iii).
152. 11(e)(3)(iii).
153. 11(e)(3)(iii).
154. 11(c)(2)(iv).
155. 11(c)(2)(iv).

2

Included and Excluded Property

2.1 Introduction

If a taxpayer elects to come within the provision of the Class Life ADR System of depreciation, some assets must be included, other assets must be excluded, and still other assets may be included or excluded at the option of the taxpayer. The purpose of this chapter is to examine these three categories of property.

2.2 Excluded Property

The primary requirements for eligibility of an asset to utilize the Class Life ADR System are that the asset must be depreciable and must be tangible.[1] Thus, land is excluded because it is not depreciable, while patents are excluded because they are not tangible.

There are three additional qualification requirements. First, there must be an asset guideline class[2] and an asset guideline period[3] for the asset for the year in which Class Life ADR depreciation is elected.[4] Second, the asset must have been placed in service[5] by the taxpayer in 1971 or thereafter.[6] A transitional rule excludes property acquired by a related entity prior to 1971 and subsequently transferred to the taxpayer.[7] Assets placed in service before 1971 can qualify for the

Guideline Class Life System of depreciation.[8] Third, included assets must constitute either "Section 1245 property"[9] (generally personal property) or "Section 1250 property"[10] (generally real estate excluding land) to be eligible for Class Life ADR depreciation.[11] However, almost all tangible depreciable assets are in either category. Somewhat different eligibility rules apply to public utilities.[12]

Thus, an asset that fails any one of the two initial tests or three subsequent tests must be excluded from the Class Life ADR System. Such an asset would be depreciated on the basis of facts and circumstances, as if the Class Life ADR System did not exist.

2.3 Mandatory and Optional Inclusion

Once it has been determined that an asset is not within one of the five categories of exclusion discussed in *Section 2.2*, the asset must be included within the Class Life ADR depreciation system if the system is elected for the taxable year,[13] unless a specific optional exclusion applies. Thus, unless such an optional exclusion is applicable, all eligible property first placed in service during the taxable year of election must be included, whether placed in service in a trade or business or held for production of income.[14] The Regulations provide for the following optional exclusions from the Class Life ADR System:[15]

1. Used property
2. Property receiving the old investment credit
3. Amortization property and special depreciation property
4. Real property
5. Subsidiary assets

These exclusions will be analyzed in *Sections 2.4–2.8* of this chapter.

2.4 Used Property

The used property rule gives taxpayers the option of excluding previously used property from the Class Life ADR System. This exclusion is sought and utilized by many taxpayers because they can (or think they can) justify a useful life for these assets which is shorter than the minimum of the asset depreciation range.

Used property may be excluded only if there is no specific used-property asset guideline class for the assets.[16] As of the date of this writing, no such used property classes have been established, so all used property is potentially eligible for exclusion.

The used-property rule is a 10-percent rule. Used property eligible for the exclusion, as determined in the preceding paragraph, must exceed 10 percent of all property placed in service that year.[17] In applying this test, all assets are measured by their unadjusted basis,[18] which is generally the original cost to the taxpayer. Assets are grouped into two categories, Section 1245 property[19] and Section 1250 property,[20] and the 10-percent rule applies separately to each. If the used-property test is met for a category of property (Section 1245 property or Section 1250 property), a taxpayer may exclude all, but not less than all, used property in that category.[21] This test is applied each year to assets placed in service that year.[22] The following example illustrates the application of the used-property rule:

	Section 1245 Property	Section 1250 Property
Total purchases	$1,500,000	$3,500,000
Used property acquired	$ 135,000	$ 420,000
Percentage	9	12
Eligible for exclusion	$ 0	$ 420,000

The used-property rule contains special definitions of the term "used property." In general, used property means property of which the taxpayer was not the original user.[23] However, two categories of property are treated as used for purposes of the 10-percent test, even though under other rules they might be treated as new:[24] eligible used property subject to special depreciation or amortization,[25] and eligible used property acquired in a transaction producing a carryover of tax attributes.[26]

It is also important to note that, assuming the used property is not excluded altogether, these used assets cannot be placed in the same vintage account as new assets.[27]

2.5 Property Subject to the Old Investment Credit

The investment credit had been repealed by the Tax Reform Act of 1969 for property acquired after April 18, 1969, unless a special transitional rule was applicable. The investment credit was later restored as part of the Revenue Act of 1971. During the hiatus between repeal and restoration, recapture of prior year's investment credit could be avoided by acquiring replacement property,[28] some of which might have been acquired during 1971 prior to the effective date of the investment credit restoration but after the effective date of the Class Life ADR System. Such assets could be excluded from the

Class Life ADR System at the option of the taxpayer, and all or less than all could be excluded. To be eligible for the exclusion, the acquired assets must replace investment credit property disposed of prior to August 15, 1971, and the replacement property must be ineligible for the new investment credit.[29] Very few assets came within this optional exclusion.

When the investment credit was repealed in 1969, transition rules enabled limited acquisitions subsequent to that date to qualify for the credit. Some of these acquisitions may have been made in 1971 or later and thus would come within the scope of the Class Life ADR System.[30] Most of these acquisitions are eligible for the restored investment credit, but some are not. These latter assets may be excluded from the Class Life ADR System.[31] Very few assets come within the scope of this optional exclusion, though it does apply to storage facilities that are not used for the bulk storage of tangible commodities.

2.6 Amortization Property and Special Depreciation Property

The Internal Revenue Code authorizes seven types of special amortization in lieu of conventional depreciation:

1. Depreciation of expenditures to rehabilitate low-income rental housing.[32]
2. Amortization of pollution-control facilities.[33,*]
3. Amortization of railroad rolling stock.[34]
4. Amortization of railroad grading and tunnel bores.[35]
5. Amortization of coal-mine safety equipment.[36]
6. Amortization of on-the-job training and child-care facilities,[37,†]
7. Amortization of improvements by a lessee on the lessor's property.[38]

The amortization provisions enable the assets in question to be amortized on a straight-line basis over a 60-month period, except for railroad grading and tunnel bores where the period is 50 years and for leasehold improvements where the term is frequently the leasehold period. Consequently, rapid amortization is frequently preferable to depreciation under the Class Life ADR System. To enable taxpayers using Class Life ADR depreciation to obtain these amortization bene-

---

*Feinschreiber, "Federal Tax Incentives for Pollution Control," *The New York Certified Public Accountant,* October 1970, pp. 803–808.

†Feinschreiber, "Child Care Facilities—Some Unanswered Questions," *Taxes,* August 1972, pp. 453–458.

fits, the Regulations enable a taxpayer to exclude assets subject to rapid amortization.[39]

In the case of the first five types of rapid amortization, the amortization may be elected for a year following the year in which the asset is placed in service. If such property has been initially subject to Class Life ADR depreciation, election of rapid amortization will cause termination of the Class Life ADR provisions applicable to these assets.[40] The termination date is the beginning of the taxable year for which the rapid amortization is computed.[41] Termination also causes an adjustment of the balances in the vintage account from which the asset is removed. Consequently, the unadjusted basis of the property is removed, as of the termination date, from the unadjusted basis of the vintage account.[42] The depreciation reserve for the vintage account is reduced by the depreciation attributable to the property now being amortized.[43] Salvage value for the account may be reduced by the amount of salvage where attributable to the removed asset.[44] Such a removal of an asset from a vintage account does not affect depreciation for prior years under the Class Life ADR System.[45]

In some situations, a taxpayer may desire to exclude certain otherwise includible assets from the Class Life ADR System. Usually, the taxpayer would seek the exclusion when a method such as units of production or machine hours would provide more rapid depreciation. If the conditions specified in the following paragraph are met, the assets may be excluded.

To obtain this exclusion, a taxpayer must use depreciation methods, other than the accepted time-based methods, for at least 75 percent of the guideline class assets acquired that year.[46] Secondly, the taxpayer must agree to continue to use these methods until the Internal Revenue Service consents to a change in method.[47] It is uncertain whether this latter provision supersedes the automatic permission to switch from the unit-of-production method to the straight-line method.[48] If these conditions are met, all (but not less than all) property in the guideline class acquired during the taxable year is excluded from the Class Life ADR System.[49]

2.7 Real Property (Section 1250 Property)

Buildings and other Section 1250 property can be excluded from the Class Life ADR election until the Treasury promulgates class lives for real property and these lives become effective.[50]

The Revenue Act of 1971 contained a temporary exclusion for real property to enable the Treasury to study its inclusion into the Class Life ADR System.[51] The exclusion was scheduled to terminate at the end of 1973, but the Treasury study had not been completed at that time, leaving many taxpayers in limbo during 1974. The Senate Finance Committee was concerned that premature inclusion of real estate would "unfavorably disturb" the remainder of the Class Life ADR System.[52] Consequently, the exclusion for real property was extended.

There is an important difference between the original real estate exclusion measure and the new statute: The 1971 exclusion required the taxpayer to justify a shorter life for the real property under the old Guideline rules, including the Reserve Ratio test but not the "minimal adjustment" provision.[53] Now a taxpayer can determine useful life of real property placed in service in 1974 or afterward on the basis of facts and circumstances.[54]

If a building is excluded under this provision, the elevators and escalators in the building are also excluded from the Class Life ADR System.[55] Once the life is justified under the rule described in the preceding paragraph, that life will be treated as being justified for future years.[56] Consequently, it appears that this justified life can be used for all purposes, including the computation of depreciation deductions.

2.8 Subsidiary Assets

Subsidiary assets are items such as jigs, dies, molds, returnable containers, glassware, silverware, textile mill cam assemblies, and other items treated as subsidiary assets under the old Guideline rules.[57] A further requirement for subsidiary asset categorization is that such items must be usually and properly accounted for separately from other property and that the depreciation method not be expressed in terms of years.[58]

A taxpayer may exclude subsidiary assets from the Class Life ADR System if two requirements are met.[59] First, eligible subsidiary assets must constitute at least 3 percent of the assets in a guideline class, measured by unadjusted basis.[60] Second, the subsidiary assets must be placed in service before the effective date of a supplemental guideline class for the subsidiary assets,[61] or before January 1, 1974.[62]

As of this writing, 11 supplemental guideline classes have been publicly issued for subsidiary assets, though others may have been issued privately to industry groups, while still others are under consideration by the Internal Revenue Service.[63] The subsidiary asset guideline classes that have been officially promulgated pertain to special tools. These classes are presented in the accompanying table.

For other taxpayers, it is conceivable that subsidiary assets may be

Supplemental Classes for Special Tools

Class	Items Manufactured by Machines in Class	Asset Guideline Period (Years)
20.50	Food and beverages	4.0
30.11	Rubber products	4.0
30.21	Plastic products	3.5
33.11	Primary ferrous metals	6.5
33.21	Primary nonferrous metals	6.5
34.01	Fabricated metal products	3.0
35.11	Metalworking machines	6.0
35.21	Other machines	6.5
36.11	Electrical equipment	5.0
37.12	Motor vehicles	3.0
37.33	Ships and boats	6.5

exluded automatically from the Class Life ADR election on the basis that there is no applicable guideline class. However, support for this position is tenuous.

Note that if the election to exclude subsidiary assets is made, all subsidiary assets in the guideline class acquired during that taxable year must be excluded.[64]

2.9 Carryover Rules—Acquisitions from Affiliates

The Class Life ADR Regulations contain safeguards to prevent assets acquired before 1971 from coming within the scope of these provisions and achieving a 20-percent reduction in asset life. The specific rule prohibiting devices to "reacquire" previously acquired assets declares that property acquired "by reason of a mere change in the form of conducting a trade or business" is ineligible.[65] Moreover, "mere change in form" is given an extremely broad interpretation in the Regulations.

A "mere change in form" is considered to take place if either of two conditions apply:

1. If the transferor retains a substantial interest in the trade or business, there is a mere change in form.[66] Similarly, if the transferor is a partnership, estate, trust, or corporation, the transfer is considered a mere change in form if the partners, beneficiaries, or shareholders retain a substantial interest in the trade or business.[67] Retention of a substantial interest is measured in relation to the total interests of all persons in the trade or business.[68] "Substantial interest" is otherwise undefined.

2. A mere change in form takes place where the property receives a carryover basis when transferred. In more technical terms, this rule

means that the property in the hands of the transferee is determined in whole or in part by reference to the basis of the property in the hands of the transferor.[69]

The Regulations provide two examples of mere change in form in which the assets do not become eligible for the Class Life ADR System: transfer to a corporation in the same affiliated group,[70] and transfer to a controlled corporation.[71]

These exclusionary rules apply only where the transferor acquired the property before 1971.[72] A reverse rule applies to the transfer of assets that were subject to Class Life ADR depreciation in the hands of the transferor.[73] If there is a carryover of tax attributes to the transferee,[74] the transferee must utilize the Class Life ADR depreciation system.[75]

When a transferee is required to utilize the Class Life ADR depreciation system because it was used by the transferor, four specific carryover rules apply:

1. The transferee must use a guideline class as nearly coextensive as possible with the guideline class of the transferor.[76]

2. The transferee must place the assets in vintage accounts by year of the transferor's acquisition.[77]

3. The same asset depreciation period must be used.[78]

4. The same depreciation method must be used unless one of the automatic changes in depreciation method is applicable[79] or permission to change depreciation methods is obtained from the Internal Revenue Service.[80]

If the transferor did not elect the Class Life ADR System, or if the transferor did not include these assets within the election, the transferee may not include them within its use of the Class Life ADR System.[81]

REFERENCES

1. 11(b)(2).
2. 11(b)(4)(i).
3. 11(b)(4)(i).
4. 11(b)(4)(ii), 11(b)(2)(i).
5. 11(e)(1).
6. 11(b)(2)(ii).
7. 11(b)(7).
8. 12(a)(1).
9. Section 1245(a)(3).
10. Section 1250(c).
11. 11(b)(2)(iii).
12. 11(b)(6), Section 167(l)(3)(A).
13. 11(b)(5)(ii).
14. 11(b)(5)(ii).
15. 11(b)(5)(ii).
16. 11(b)(5)(iii)(a), 11(b)(5)(iii)(b), 11(b)(5)(iii)(c).
17. 11(b)(5)(iii)(a), 11(b)(5)(iii)(b).
18. 11(b)(5)(iii)(a), 11(b)(5)(iii)(b).
19. 11(b)(5)(iii)(a).
20. 11(b)(5)(iii)(b).
21. 11(b)(5)(iii)(a), 11(b)(5)(iii)(b).
22. 11(b)(5)(iii)(a), 11(b)(5)(iii)(b).
23. 11(b)(5)(iii)(c).

24. 11(b)(5)(iii)(c).
25. 11(b)(5)(iii)(c)(1), 11(b)(5)(v)(a).
26. 11(b)(5)(iii)(c)(2), Section 381(a).
27. 11(b)(3)(ii).
28. Section 47(a)(5)(B), Section 38, Section 49.
29. 11(b)(5)(iv)(b), Section 50.
30. Section 38, Section 48(a), Section 49, Section 50.
31. 11(b)(5)(iv)(a).
32. Section 167(k).
33. Section 169.
34. Section 184.
35. Section 185.
36. Section 187.
37. Section 188.
38. Reg. Sec. 1.162–11(b).
39. 11(b)(5)(v)(b).
40. 11(b)(5)(v)(b).
41. 11(b)(5)(v)(b).
42. 11(b)(5)(v)(b).
43. 11(c)(1)(v)(b), 11(b)(5)(v)(b).
44. 11(d)(3)(vii)(e), 11(b)(5)(v)(b).
45. 11(b)(5)(v)(b).
46. 11(b)(5)(v)(b)(1).
47. 11(b)(5)(v)(b)(2), Form 3115.
48. Rev. Proc. 74–11, Section 4.01(d), 1974 I.R.B. 21.
49. 11(b)(5)(v)(b).
50. P.L. 93–625 (January 3, 1975), Sec. 5(a).
51. P.L. 92–178, Sec. 109(e)(1).
52. Report No. 93–1357, to accompany H.R. 421 (December 16, 1974).
53. Rev. Proc. 62–21 as amended; Rev. Proc. 65–13, Section 4, Part II.
54. P.L. 93–625 (January 3, 1975), Sec. 5(a)(2); Sec. 5(d).
55. 11(b)(5)(vi)(a).
56. 11(b)(5)(vi)(b).
57. Rev. Proc. 62–21, Group One, Class 5, 11(b)(5)(vii).
58. 11(b)(5)(vii).
59. 11(b)(5)(vii).
60. 11(b)(5)(vii)(a).
61. 11(b)(5)(vii)(b)(1).
62. 11(b)(5)(vii)(b)(2).
63. Rev. Proc. 73–25, 1973–40 I.R.B. 13; Rev. Proc. 74–30, T.I.R. 1300, August 23, 1974.
64. 11(b)(5)(vii).
65. 11(b)(7).
66. 11(b)(7)(i).
67. 11(b)(7)(i).
68. 11(b)(7).
69. 11(b)(7)(ii).
70. Section 1504(a), 11(b)(7) Example (1).
71. Section 351, 11(b)(7) Example (2).
72. 11(b)(7).
73. 11(e)(3)(i)(a).
74. Section 381(a).
75. 11(e)(3)(i).
76. 11(e)(3)(i)(b).
77. 11(e)(3)(i)(b).
78. 11(e)(3)(i)(b).
79. 11(c)(1)(iii).
80. 11(e)(3)(i)(b).
81. 11(e)(3)(i)(c).

3

Depreciation Methods

3.1 Introduction to Depreciation Methods

The U.S. tax law allows a variety of tax depreciation methods. These methods and their use do not depend on the election or nonelection of Class Life ADR depreciation. However, these methods are applied in a somewhat different manner if Class Life ADR depreciation is elected. These differences may affect the decision to elect or not to elect Class Life ADR depreciation. Correspondingly, the election or nonelection of Class Life ADR depreciation may affect depreciation method selection.

This chapter discusses the various depreciation methods and eligibility requirements for their use. Then, the most important methods are examined in detail, depreciation method switching is considered, and the optimal selection of depreciation methods is examined.

3.2 Available Depreciation Methods

Depreciation methods are the means for allocating the cost of an asset to various future time periods. There are basically two types of depreciation methods, those based on physical units and those based on time.

The depreciation methods based on physical units are essentially of two types, units of production and machine-hours. These methods have an important difference. The units-of-production method mea-

25

sures output, while the machine-hours method in essence measures input. Both require an educated guess as to the future use of the asset. This estimate is difficult to make, largely because economic obsolescence must be taken into account along with physical deterioration.

These methods have declined in usefulness and in use because they produce little if any acceleration. Rather, these methods tend to allocate the purchase price in a relatively linear manner, with equal amounts assigned to each applicable time period. In this regard, the units-of-production method appears to be preferable to the machine-hours method in that it recognizes the declining productivity of the machine.

These two methods of depreciation have an additional major drawback: Both require cumbersome recordkeeping. Of the two methods, machine-hour depreciation is easier to apply because time is easier to measure than output. In fact, the units-of-production method may be inapplicable in various circumstances because of the lack of discrete output necessary if records are to be kept. This problem is least likely to occur when a cost-center accounting system is used, somewhat more likely under a process cost system, and quite likely in a job-order situation.

Time-based depreciation methods now predominate. These methods apportion the purchase price to various years in the future. The time period used for this purpose is generally the useful life of the asset or some function of the useful life.

There are three fundamental time-based methods that are discussed in subsequent sections of this chapter: straight line (SL), sum of the years-digits (SYD), and declining balance (DB) at various rates.

In relatively rare situations, still other depreciation methods may be applied. The base stock method, in which amounts acquired in excess of the "base stock" for an asset are written off as current period expense while the base stock is not depreciated, finds little use because it is not accepted by the Internal Revenue Service. There is a special railroad retirement method applicable only to railroads. Still another method generates smaller depreciation in earlier years, with the bulk of the depreciation saved until the asset is near retirement. Because these methods are rarely used, they will not be discussed further in this book.

Not all depreciation methods mentioned in the preceding paragraphs are available for all assets. The physical-units methods can be used where appropriate, that is, where justified on the basis of facts and circumstances. Of the time-based methods, only straight line may be used as a matter of right. Sum of the years-digits and declining balance (at various rates) may be used only as permitted by statute.

Whenever a declining balance depreciation method is permissible, a taxpayer may select a rate less than the maximum allowable, though it is rarely advantageous to do so.

The sum of the years-digits (SYD) method and the double declining balance (DDB) method may be used only for assets that constitute new tangible personal property having a life of 3 years or more,[1] new residential rental real property,[2] or new commercial or industrial real property either constructed or acquired before July 25, 1969, or subject to a special transitional rule.[3,*]

The 150-percent declining balance method can be utilized for used personal property having a life of 3 years or more,[4] for used real estate acquired before July 25, 1969,[5] and for new commercial and industrial real estate acquired or constructed after July 24, 1969.[6]

The 125-percent declining balance method may be utilized for used residential real estate acquired after July 24, 1969, provided the property has a useful life of 20 years or longer.[7]

When these accelerated depreciation methods are not available, the straight-line method may be used.

Some of the depreciation methods described above were not available for certain property acquired during parts of 1966 and 1967.[8] Also, these depreciation methods were generally unavailable for property acquired prior to 1954.[9] In certain situations described above, the availability of an accelerated depreciation method depends upon the property's being new. In more technical terms, *new* property means property where the original use commences with the taxpayer.[10] The term "original use" means the first use to which the property is put, whether or not such use corresponds to such use of the property by the taxpayer.[11] This rule also is specifically applicable when the Class Life ADR depreciation system is elected.[12]

Generally, the same restrictions on the use of accelerated depreciation methods apply when the Class Life ADR system is elected.[13] All property in a single vintage account must be depreciated by the same depreciation method,[14] so that when similar property is acquired but some assets are new while others are used, separate vintage accounts must be utilized for the new and used assets. Similarly, property that does not have a useful life of three years or more cannot be included in a vintage account for which accelerated depreciation is to be used.[15] If such property is included in the account, accelerated depreciation may not be utilized for the account.[16]

When depreciation is based on the Class Life ADR System, unless accelerated depreciation is prohibited or limited to 125 percent declin-

*Feinschreiber, "When to Switch Depreciation Methods for Real Estate," 1 *Journal of Real Estate Taxation* 131 (1974).

ing balance in the case of real estate,[17] all assets in a class may be grouped together and depreciated under 150 percent declining balance depreciation.[18] Generally, however, this latter alternative is not advantageous.

3.3 The Straight-Line Method

The straight-line (SL) depreciation method allocates the amount that is ultimately depreciable over the life of the asset. Each taxable year receives a proportionate amount of the depreciation. For each full taxable year in which an asset is in service, the depreciation charges will be equal.[19]

If the Class Life ADR depreciation system is not elected or is not available for the assets, the amount depreciable (described in the preceding paragraph) is basis less the salvage value.[20] If Class Life ADR depreciation is utilized, salvage value does not reduce annual depreciation. Instead, salvage value comes into play only when the depreciable amount (basis less salvage value) has been exhausted.[21] The following example illustrates this difference. Here, the basis is $9,000, the salvage value after the Section 167(f) reduction is $3,000, and the useful life is 3 years.

Year	Class Life ADR Depreciation	Conventional Depreciation	Difference
1	$3,000	$2,000	$1,000
2	3,000	2,000	1,000
3	0	2,000	−2,000
Total	$6,000	$6,000	$ 0

Thus, the Class Life ADR System provides some acceleration to straight-line depreciation.

In mathematical terms, the annual depreciation formulas under each system can be expressed as follows, when L is the useful life, B is the basis, S is the salvage value, and D is the annual depreciation charge:

$$D = \frac{B - S}{L} \quad \text{under conventional depreciation}$$

$$D = \frac{B}{L} \quad \text{under Class Life ADR}$$

The straight-line depreciation rate, $1/L$, can also be expressed as a percentage. This percentage is used for multiple-asset open end accounts when the Class Life ADR System is not utilized.[22] Note that actual proceeds from retired assets do not affect the annual depreciation charges.[23]

3.4 Sum of the Years-Digits

The sum of the years-digits (SYD) depreciation method is applicable whether or not the Class Life ADR System is utilized. There are important differences in application. These differences will be discussed at the end of this section. First, the computational aspects of sum of the years-digits depreciation are presented.

The sum of the years-digits method places most of an asset's depreciation in the early years of the asset's life, as Table 2 illustrates.*

The sum of the years-digits method first requires that the asset life be expressed in whole numbers of years. Then an arithmetic series of natural numbers is created and the sum of the series is determined by addition. This sum serves as the denominator for each year. The numerators are the numbers in the series, taken in descending order. The computation below demonstrates this technique for an asset with a four-year life. D_1, D_2, D_3, and D_4 represent the depreciation for various years during the life of the asset.

$$\text{Arithmetic series: } 1, 2, 3, 4$$
$$\text{Sum of series: } 10$$
$$D_1 = {}^4\!/_{10}$$
$$D_2 = {}^3\!/_{10}$$
$$D_3 = {}^2\!/_{10}$$
$$D_4 = {}^1\!/_{10}$$

TABLE 2

Asset Life (Years)	Percent of Depreciable Amount Depreciated During First Quarter of Life	Percent of Depreciable Amount Depreciated During First Half of Life
4	40.00	70.00
8	41.67	72.22
12	42.31	73.08
16	42.65	73.53
20	42.86	73.81
24	43.00	74.00
40	43.24	74.39
60	43.44	74.59
80	43.52	74.69
100	43.56	74.75
Infinity	43.75	75.00

*Feinschreiber, "Accelerated Depreciation: A Proposed New Method," 7 *University of Chicago-London School of Economics Journal of Accounting Research* 17 (1969).

Where an asset has a long useful life, this computation can be facilitated by using a mathematical formula. The denominator is generated by the formula for the sum of an arithmetic series, in which L is the useful life:

$$\frac{L(L+1)}{2}$$

The numerators are represented by the following formula, in which Y is the year for which depreciation is computed:

$$L - Y + 1$$

Consequently, the entered formula becomes

$$D_y = \frac{L - Y + 1}{[L(L+1)]/2}$$

The Class Life ADR depreciation system, by virtue of the depreciation range, has introduced lives that are not integers but are integers plus a half-year.[24] Here the computation of sum of the years-digits depreciation is similar. If an asset has a life of 5.5 years, the denominator is $5.5 + 4.5 + 3.5 + 2.5 + 1.5 + 0.5 = 18$, and the annual depreciation fractions are $^{5.5}\!/_{18}$, $^{4.5}\!/_{18}$, and so forth. The mathematical formula for computing the annual depreciation charge is:

$$D_y = \frac{L - Y + 1}{\frac{1}{2}(L + \frac{1}{2})^2}$$

Conventional depreciation and the Class Life ADR System each have specific requirements for the application of sum of the years-digits depreciation. The remaining paragraphs in this section describe these requirements.

If the Class Life ADR System is not elected, salvage value must be deducted from the basis of the asset to determine the depreciable base.[25] If the Class Life ADR System is utilized, salvage value does not affect annual depreciation charges but merely serves to limit total depreciation.[26] Consequently, sum of the years-digits depreciation receives some acceleration under the Class Life ADR System.

The difference in computation between Class Life ADR depreciation and conventional depreciation is illustrated in the example that follows on the next page, where basis is $10,000 and salvage value after the Section 167(f) reduction is $1,000.

If the useful life of an asset is changed, which may happen if the Class Life ADR System is not elected, sum of the years-digits depre-

Year	Class Life ADR	Conventional	Difference
1	$4,000	$3,600	$400
2	3,000	2,700	300
3	2,000	1,800	200
4	0	900	−900
Total	$9,000	$9,000	$ 0

ciation is computed in the following manner: For the year in which the change is made, the change takes place as of the beginning of the year.[27] The unrecovered basis at that time, less salvage value, is then used for future computations.[28] However, salvage value may itself be adjusted.[29] Thus, if depreciation is based on a 10-year life, and at the end of 5 years' depreciation the remaining life is determined to be 7 years, the fraction for the first year after the change (year 6) is $7/28$.

There is an additional technique for computing sum of the years-digits depreciation—the remaining-life approach. Here, the denominator declines along with the numerator, and this fraction is applied to the remaining depreciable base rather than to the original depreciation base. More specifically, each year the denominator becomes the sum of an arithmetic series with one less term.

Where an asset has a 4-year life, $10,000 cost, and zero salvage value, the remaining-life computation would work as follows:

$$4/10 \times \$10,000 = \$4,000$$
$$3/6 \times \ \ \$6,000 = \$3,000$$
$$2/3 \times \ \ \$3,000 = \$2,000$$
$$1/1 \times \ \ \$1,000 = \$1,000$$

The mathematic formula for the remaining-life fraction is

$$D_y = \frac{2}{L - Y + 2}$$

This fraction is to be multiplied by the remaining depreciable base. The Regulations provide a more complicated formula for the remaining-life computation, which takes into account remaining lives that are not integers.

The conventional depreciation regulations describe the remaining-life method of computation,[30] and provide a table in tenths of a year from 100 years down to 1 year.[31] If the remaining life is less than 1 year, the full depreciation base is equal to the amount of depreciation for the taxable year.

The remaining-life plan may not be used under the Class Life ADR System.[32] In conventional (facts and circumstances) depreciation, the remaining-life plan may be used, at the option of the taxpayer, for item accounts (individual assets).[33] For multiple-asset accounts, whether group, classified, or composite, the remaining-life plan must be used if the Class Life ADR System is not elected, unless the Internal Revenue Service gives permission to use another method for computing sum of the years-digits depreciation.[34]

Computation of sum of the years-digits depreciation under the remaining-life plan for multiple-asset accounts is quite complex, particularly where the accounts are open-ended, that is, where acquisitions in later years are added to the same accounts, or where classified or composite accounts are used. Here, the remaining life for each component must be determined and then averaged.[35] This computation usually involves a division of the unrecovered cost or other basis of the account, as computed by straight-line depreciation, by the gross cost or other basis of the account, followed by multiplication of this amount by the average life of the assets in the account.[36]

Complexity is compounded by the fact that Rev. Proc. 65-13 did not permit use of the Guideline system where open-end accounts are utilized for sum of the years-digits depreciation. As a result, many taxpayers have one account for earlier acquisitions and separate accounts for acquisitions in each subsequent year.

Salvage value is not a factor for determining remaining useful life.[37]

If Class Life ADR depreciation is elected, salvage value does not affect the annual depreciation computations, and the regular method for computing sum of the years-digits, rather than the remaining-life method, is to be used.[38]

Averaging conventions, described in Chapter 4, cause some difficulties in application when the sum of the years-digits depreciation method is utilized. These problems increase when Class Life ADR depreciation is elected and the useful life is a whole number plus a half; for example, $5\frac{1}{2}$ years, as Table 3 illustrates.[39,*]

TABLE 3

Years of Prior Use	Remaining Life	Asset Year	Depreciation
0	5.5	1	$5\frac{.5}{18}$
1	4.5	2	$4\frac{.5}{18}$
2	3.5	3	$3.\frac{5}{18}$
3	2.5	4	$2\frac{.5}{18}$
4	1.5	5	$1.\frac{5}{18}$
5	0.5	6	$0\frac{.5}{18}$

*Feinschreiber, "Computing Depreciation Under the 'Class Life' System," 43 *CPA Journal* 857 (1973).

Now assume that the half-year averaging convention is utilized, as illustrated by Table 4. The numbers in Table 4 are just the numerators. The denominator for each number is 18, as shown in Table 5.

Note in Table 3 that while the useful life is 5.5 years, it takes 7 taxable years (Tables 4 and 5) to depreciate the asset.

TABLE 4

Asset Year	Depreciation	1	2	3	4	5	6	7
1	5.5	2.75	2.75					
2	4.5	—	2.25	2.25				
3	3.5	—	—	1.75	1.75			
4	2.5	—	—	—	1.25	1.25		
5	1.5	—	—	—	—	0.75	0.75	
6	0.5	—	—	—	—	—	0.25	0.25
	18.0	2.75	5.00	4.00	3.00	2.00	1.00	0.25

TABLE 5

Taxable Year	Depreciation
1	$2.75/18$
2	$5/18$
3	$4/18$
4	$3/18$
5	$2/18$
6	$1/18$
7	$0.25/18$

3.5 Declining Balance Depreciation

The declining balance depreciation method applies a constant depreciation rate to a declining balance. The rate is a percentage of the straight-line rate; for example, 125, 150, or 200 percent. Consequently, the declining balance method comprises three separate but similar depreciation computations: 200 percent declining balance (double declining balance), 150 percent declining balance, and 125 percent declining balance.

The depreciable base declines each year by an amount equal to the prior year's depreciation. The following formula can be used to compute declining balance depreciation:

$$D_1 = \frac{P}{L}$$

$$B_1 = 1 - \frac{P}{L}$$

$$D_2 = \left(1 - \frac{P}{L}\right)\frac{P}{L}$$

$$B_2 = \left(1 - \frac{P}{L}\right) - \left(1 - \frac{P}{L}\right)\frac{P}{L}$$

$$= \left(1 - \frac{P}{L}\right)\left(1 - \frac{P}{L}\right)$$

$$= \left(1 - \frac{P}{L}\right)^2$$

$$D_3 = \left(1 - \frac{P}{L}\right)^2 \frac{P}{L}$$

$$B_3 = \left(1 - \frac{P}{L}\right)^2 - \left(1 - \frac{P}{L}\right)^2 \frac{P}{L}$$

$$= \left(1 - \frac{P}{L}\right)^2 \left(1 - \frac{P}{L}\right)$$

$$= \left(1 - \frac{P}{L}\right)^3$$

where D = depreciation for a particular year
B = adjusted basis at end of year
P = declining balance percentage (for example, 125, 150, or 200 percent)
L = useful life of asset
Y = particular year in the life of the asset[*]
In general,

$$D_Y = \left(1 - \frac{P}{L}\right)^{Y-1} \frac{P}{L}$$

$$B_Y = \left(1 - \frac{P}{L}\right)^Y$$

The following example illustrates the declining balance method when an asset has a 3-year life and the rate is twice the straight-line rate.

$$D_1 = \frac{2}{3}$$
$$B_1 = 1 - \frac{2}{3} = \frac{1}{3}$$
$$D_2 = \frac{1}{3} \times \frac{2}{3} = \frac{2}{9}$$
$$B_2 = \frac{1}{3} - \frac{2}{9} = \frac{1}{9}$$
$$D_3 = \frac{1}{9} \times \frac{2}{3} = \frac{2}{27}$$
$$B_3 = \frac{1}{9} - \frac{2}{27} = \frac{1}{27}$$

[*]Feinschreiber, "The Impact of High Salvage Value on Double Declining Balance Depreciation," 20 *South Carolina Law Review* 47 (1968).

TABLE 6

Life	Remainder, as a Percentage of Basis	Life	Remainder, as a Percentage of Basis
3	3.704	20	12.158
4	6.250	21	12.224
5	7.776	22	12.284
6	8.779	23	12.340
7	9.486	24	12.390
8	10.011	25	12.436
9	10.416	30	12.621
10	10.737	33	12.704
11	10.999	40	12.851
12	11.216	50	12.989
13	11.398	60	13.079
14	11.554	70	13.145
15	11.689	80	13.194
16	11.807	90	13.231
17	11.910	100	13.262
18	12.002	Infinity	13.534
19	12.084		

As this example illustrates, an asset is not depreciated at the end of its useful life when the declining balance method is used. Rather, there is an undepreciated remainder. Table 6 illustrates the undepreciated remainder for various lives when the depreciation rate is twice the straight-line rate (double declining balance).

Some basic rules for applying declining balance depreciation are applicable whether or not Class Life ADR depreciation is elected.[40]

Because declining balance depreciation leaves an automatic remainder, and this remainder is supposed to represent salvage value,[41] the annual depreciation charges are not reduced to any extent by estimated salvage value,[42] as the table below illustrates for an asset with a cost of $2,700, useful life of 3 years, and various salvage values.

Year	Salvage $100	Salvage $300	Salvage $900
1	1,800	1,800	1,800
2	600	600	0
3	200	0	0

In contrast, actual salvage value proceeds are added to the depreciation reserve along with accumulated depreciation.[43] Depreciation

TABLE 7

Asset Life	Percentage of Cost Depreciated During First Quarter of Life	Percentage of Cost Depreciated During First Half of Life
4	50.00	75.00
8	43.75	68.36
12	42.13	66.51
16	41.38	65.64
20	40.95	65.13
24	40.67	64.80
40	40.13	64.15
60	39.86	63.83
80	39.73	63.68
100	39.65	63.58
Infinity	39.35	63.21

is based on cost or other basis less the reserve, so actual salvage value proceeds reduce depreciation in future years.

The general rule that an asset may not be depreciated below salvage value is applicable to declining balance depreciation.[44] The Section 167(f) salvage value reduction may be applicable, however.

When the Class Life ADR depreciation system is not utilized, the useful life may be extended and salvage value may be adjusted.[45] If the useful life is changed, subsequent computations are made as if the revised useful life had originally been estimated.[46] Thus, the subsequent rate is based on the revised useful life.[47] For example, if a life of 10 years had been used, and 6 years had elapsed, but the remaining life is revised upward from 4 years to 6 years, the total life is 12 years, so the rate is $16^{2}/_3$ percent if double declining balance depreciation is utilized.[48]

When double declining balance depreciation is utilized, significant acceleration results, at least for short-lived assets,* as Table 7 indicates.†

3.6 The Depreciation Reserve

Every item or account undergoing depreciation must have a depreciation reserve. This general requirement applies whether or not Class Life ADR depreciation is elected. However, the Class Life ADR

---

*Feinschreiber, "From the Thoughtful Tax Man," *Taxes,* November 1973, pp. 680–681.

†Feinschreiber, "Accelerated Depreciation: A Proposed New Method," 7 *University of Chicago-London School of Economics Journal of Accounting Research* 17 (1969).

System includes specific requirements for the depreciation reserve. These requirements are discussed in the subsequent paragraphs.

Each vintage account must have a separate reserve, which must be reflected on the tax return.[49] The reserve consists of accumulated depreciation together with numerous adjustments.[50] Briefly, these rules are:

1. In the case of ordinary retirements, all proceeds are added to the reserve.[51] The unadjusted basis of the asset is not removed from the asset account and no adjustment is made to the reserve.[52]

2. In the case of ordinary retirements other than by transfers to supplies or scrap, if salvage value for the account is reduced by the salvage value attributable to the retired asset, this latter amount is not added to the reserve.[53] However, in the case of transfers to supplies or scrap, salvage value is added to the reserve to the extent that the assets acquire a basis in the supplies or scrap account.[54]

3. If assets are valued upon transfer to a supplies or scrap account, the greater of the amount subtracted from the salvage value for the account or the value of the assets must be added to the reserve.[55]

4. In the case of extraordinary retirements, the reserve is reduced by the depreciation attributable to the retired asset.[56] Note that certain retirements in which gain or loss is not recognized in whole or in part are treated in the same manner.[57]

5. The reserve cannot exceed the adjusted basis; if it should do so temporarily, the reserve is to be reduced and gain recognized.[58]

6. If property is removed from a vintage account because it is real property and its categorization changes;[59] rapid amortization is elected;[60] or there is a failure to normalize in the case of public utility property,[61] the reserve is reduced by depreciation allowable for the property.[62]

The Regulation also includes timing requirements for affecting these adjustments to the reserve:[63]

1. Adjustments for ordinary retirements are treated as made at the beginning of the taxable year.

2. The date of an extraordinary retirement is determined by the applicable averaging convention.

3. Adjustments to the reserve, by virtue of the transfer of assets to a supplies or scrap account, are to be treated in accordance with the preceding rules (see items 2 and 3 in the prior list and items 1 and 2 in this list).

4. When property is specially removed from a vintage account (see item 6 in the prior list), the adjustment to the reserve is made as of the beginning of the taxable year.

Where these adjustments to the reserve are significant, they can have an impact on depreciation method selection because of the different ways in which the reserve is treated under sum of the years-digits and under double declining balance depreciation. Adjustments that reduce the reserve tend to favor the double declining balance method, while adjustments that add to the reserve favor the sum of the years-digits method, other things being equal.

3.7 Depreciation Method Switching

In many situations, taxpayers find it advantageous to change depreciation methods. In some situations, the switch may be made because the combined methods yield greater acceleration of depreciation than does any one method. In other situations, depreciation methods are changed because of a change in the underlying facts pertaining to the asset or because the taxpayer has a loss and wishes to preserve depreciation.

The statute enumerates only one depreciation method switch that is presently applicable, the change from a declining balance method to the straight-line method.[64] For about 20 years, the Internal Revenue Service erroneously contended that this provision did not permit switches from the 150 percent declining balance method without its permission.[65] This erroneous interpretation was not officially corrected until July 1974.[66]

Until 1967, the Internal Revenue Service maintained a strict position against depreciation method switching. Then there was a complete reversal in policy, as evidenced by Rev. Proc. 67-40,[67] which provides a wide choice of depreciation method switches. Rev. Proc. 67-40 has now been superseded by Rev. Proc. 74-11,[68] which also provides great flexibility as to depreciation method switching. These switching rules are applicable when Class Life ADR depreciation is not elected. The Class Life ADR switching rules will be discussed subsequently.

Rev. Proc. 74-11 enumerates 11 specific depreciation method switches.[69] Most of these changes are of little applicability, except for taxpayers who want to slow down depreciation. However, one of the enumerated changes can accelerate depreciation for many taxpayers. It is possible to switch from the double declining balance method to the sum of the years-digits method. This particular switch will be discussed at the conclusion of this chapter.

The Class Life ADR depreciation system permits three and only three depreciation method switches:[70] (1) double declining balance to sum of the years-digits, (2) declining balance to straight line, and (3) sum of the years-digits to straight line. As the concluding portion of this chapter indicates, the double declining balance method coupled with a switch to the sum of the years-digits method is usually advantageous.

3.8 Optimal Depreciation Strategies

If a taxpayer has a constant effective tax rate, and salvage value can be reduced to zero under Section 167(f), it is possible to generalize about the best depreciation method or methods to use (see Figure 1 for a comparison of methods).

1. For assets eligible for sum of the years-digits (SYD) and double declining balance (DDB), begin with double declining balance and switch to sum of the years-digits. At least one, but not more than two, full taxable years should elapse before the switch is made.* This switch is preferable to the switch to straight line, even at the best point in time for switching to straight line, if such a switch is made.*

2. For assets eligible for 150 percent declining balance depreciation, that method should be used, followed by a switch to the straight-line method. The switch should be made shortly after the first third of life, not after the first half of life.†

3. For assets eligible for 125 percent declining balance depreciation, that method should be used, followed by a switch to the straight-line method shortly after the first fifth of life.†

The mathematical proof of these general rules and the techniques used is beyond the scope of this book.** The reader is cautioned that the three rules discussed above are not applicable to all taxpayers in all circumstances.

*Feinschreiber, "When to Switch Depreciation Methods for Real Estate," 1 *Journal of Real Estate Taxation* 151 (1974).

†Feinschreiber, "Selecting the Optimal Year to Switch From 150% Declining Balance Depreciation to Straight-Line Depreciation," *The Tax Adviser,* March 1973, p. 165.

**Feinschreiber, "Accelerated Depreciation: A Proposed New Method," 7 *University of Chicago-London School of Economics Journal of Accounting Research* 17 (1969); "The Impact of High Salvage Value on Double Declining Balance Depreciation," 20 *South Carolina Law Review* 47 (1968).

FIGURE 1. Comparison of depreciation methods.

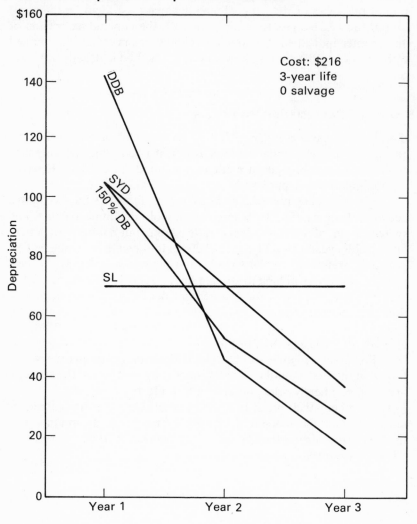

REFERENCES

1. Sec. 167(c).
2. Sec. 167(j)(2).
3. Sec. 167(j)(3).
4. Rev. Rul. 74–324, 1974–27 I.R.B.14; 11(c)(1)(iv)(*b*)(*2*).
5. Rev. Rul. 74–324, 1974–27 I.R.B.14.
6. Sec. 167(j)(1)(B).
7. Sec. 167(j)(5)(B).
8. Sec. 167(i).
9. Sec. 167(c).
10. Reg. Sec. 1.167(c)-1(a).
11. Reg. Sec. 1.167(c)-1(a).
12. 11(c)(1)(iv)(*c*).
13. 11(c)(1)(iv)(*a*).
14. 11(c)(1)(iv)(*a*).
15. 11(c)(1)(iv)(*b*)(*1*).
16. 11(c)(1)(iv)(*b*)(*1*).
17. Sec. 167(j).
18. 11(c)(1)(iv)(*b*)(*2*).
19. Reg. Sec. 1.167(b)-1(a).
20. Reg. Sec. 1.167(b)-1(a).
21. 11(c)(1)(i)(*b*).
22. Reg. Sec. 1.167(b)-1(b), Examples (2) and (3).
23. Reg. Sec. 1.167(b)-1(b), Example (3).
24. Rev. Proc. 72–10, 1971–1 CB 721; 11(c)(1)(iii)(*f*).
25. Reg. Sec. 1.167(b)-3(a)(1).
26. 11(c)(1)(i)(*c*).
27. Reg. Sec. 1.167(b)-3(a)(1)(ii).
28. Reg. Sec. 1.167(b)-3(a)(1)(ii).
29. 1(c).
30. Reg. Sec. 1.167(b)-3(a)(2)(i).
31. Reg. Sec. 1.167(b)-3(a)(2)(ii).
32. 11(c)(1)(i)(*c*).
33. Reg. Sec. 1.167(b)-3(b)(2).
34. Reg. Sec. 1.167(b)-3(b)(3).
35. Reg. Sec. 1.167(b)-3(b)(2).
36. Reg. Sec. 1.167(b)-3(b)(2).
37. Reg. Sec. 1.167(b)-3(b)(2).
38. 11(c)(1)(i)(*c*).
39. 11(c)(1)(iii)(*f*), Example (3).
40. Reg. Sec. 1.167(b)-2; 11(c)(1)(i)(*d*).
41. U.S. Code Congressional and Administrative News 4185 (1954) (House Report); U.S.Code Congressional and Administrative News 4836 (1954) (Senate Report).
42. Reg. Sec. 1.167(b)-2(a), 11(c)(1)(i)(*d*).
43. Reg. Sec. 1.167(b)-2(b), Example (2), 11(c)(1)(ii).
44. Reg. Sec. 1.167(b)-2(a), 11(c)(1)(i)(*d*).
45. 1(c).
46. Reg. Sec. 1.167(b)-2(c).
47. Reg. Sec. 1.167(b)-2(c).
48. Reg. Sec. 1.167(b)-2(c).
49. 11(c)(1)(ii).
50. 11(c)(1)(ii).
51. 11(d)(3)(iii).
52. 11(d)(3)(iii).
53. 11(d)(3)(vii)(*d*)(*1*).
54. 11(d)(3)(vii)(*d*)(*2*).
55. 11(d)(3)(viii)(*b*).
56. 11(d)(3)(iv).
57. 11(d)(3)(v).
58. 11(d)(3)(ix)(*a*).
59. 11(b)(4)(iii)(*e*).
60. 11(b)(5)(v)(*b*).
61. 11(b)(6).
62. 11(c)(1)(ii).
63. 11(c)(1)(ii).
64. Sec. 167(e)(1).
65. Rev. Rul. 57–510, 1957–2 CB 152.
66. Rev. Rul. 74–324, 1974–27 I.R.B. 14.
67. 1970–2 CB 674.
68. 1971–1 I.R.B. 21.
69. Rev. Proc. 74–11, Sec. 4.
70. 11(c)(iii).

4

Averaging Conventions

4.1 Introduction to Averaging Conventions

Tax depreciation theoretically begins when an asset is placed in service. Consequently, a proportionate part of one year's depreciation would be taken for the part of the year in which the asset is in service.[1] Similarly, when an asset is retired, a proportionate part of a year's depreciation would be taken for the part of the year prior to retirement.

Because assets are typically placed in service and retired on numerous dates throughout the taxable year, computation of the first year's depreciation and the last year's depreciation on an actual date of service-date-of-retirement basis would be time-consuming and cumbersome. To alleviate the need for daily computations, or computations on an asset-by-asset basis, many taxpayers have been using "averaging conventions." Averaging conventions treat acquisitions and retirements during the year as being made on a limited number of specific dates.*

Averaging conventions apply quite differently to the Class Life ADR System on one hand and facts-and-circumstances depreciation and the Guideline Class Life System on the other hand. Before

---

*Feinschreiber, "New Depreciation Regulations Alter First Year Averaging Conventions," *Massachusetts CPA Review,* July–August 1972, pp. 25–27.

turning to these technical specifics, we will examine the rules for determining when an asset is placed in service and is later retired.

4.2 Determining When an Asset Is Placed in Service

The Regulations provide that property is first placed in service when placed in a condition or state of readiness and availability for a specifically assigned function.[2] The specifically assigned function can be in a trade or business, the production of income, a tax-exempt activity, or a personal activity.[3] In general, the "placed in service" date refers to the date the property was first placed in service by the taxpayer, not by anyone else.[4] The "placed in service" date coincides with the date of eligibility for the investment credit, assuming the property is eligible.[5] Special rules, to be examined in subsequent paragraphs, apply to buildings, certain replacement parts, property improvements, excluded additions, and public utility property. These rules are designed for the Class Life ADR System and are not specifically applicable to other depreciation systems.

The date a building is placed in service generally does not depend upon the availability or utility of the machinery housed in the building. A building will ordinarily be treated as placed in service on the date its construction, reconstruction, or erection is substantially complete and the building is in a condition or state of readiness and availability.[6] This rule also applies in the case of a building that is constructed, reconstructed, or erected by or for the taxpayer and for the taxpayer's use,[7] as is the case where the taxpayer is a manufacturing company and the building is designed for the taxpayer. Thus, in the case of a factory building, such readiness and availability is determined without regard to whether the machinery or equipment that the building houses, or is intended to house, has been placed in service.[8]

An exception to the general rule for determining the date at which the building is placed in service applies in the case of a special-purpose structure.[9] When a building is essentially an item of machinery or equipment, or the use of the building is so closely related to the use of the machinery or equipment that it clearly can be expected to be replaced or retired contemporaneously with the machinery or equipment, readiness or availability of the building for use must take into account the readiness and availability of the machinery or equipment.[10]

Replacement parts that are capitalized like other assets are treated as placed in service when in a state of readiness or availability for use.

Parts do not have to be in actual use at that time. Where the cost or other basis of replacement parts is deducted as a repair expense under the repair allowance,[11] these parts are not treated as placed in service.[12] The same result should apply if replacement parts are deducted as a repair expense, even without use of the repair allowance, but the regulations are silent on this point.

Where the repair allowance is elected and the amount of eligible expenditures exceeds the repair allowance ceiling so that the excess must be capitalized as a property improvement in a special basis vintage account,[13] half the amount is treated as placed in service during the second half of the taxable year.[14] Presumably, the property improvement computation is not done on a first in, first out (FIFO) basis, with the first expenditures being eligible for the repair allowance, but a pro rata computation is made. Otherwise, all (or virtually all) property improvements would be treated as made during the last half of the year.

An excluded addition is generally treated as placed in service when its cost is paid or incurred.[15] If a property improvement is made outside the repair allowance system, it is treated in the same manner as an excluded addition.[16] If such excluded addition or property improvement is paid or incurred in a period extending beyond half a taxable year, a taxpayer may opt to treat these items as placed in service when available for use, if such treatment is consistently applied.[17]

Special rules will be prescribed for public utilities that consistently use clearing accounts.[18]

The averaging conventions do not determine when an asset is first placed in service. Rather, the averaging conventions come into play only after the date placed in service is determined.[19] Similarly, the date on which depreciation begins under a particular depreciation method, such as units of production or the retirement method, does not determine the date placed in service.[20] The purpose of this latter provision is questionable because these regulations apply only to Class Life ADR depreciation, which does not permit the use of such methods.

4.3 Time of Retirement

Under the Class Life ADR System, an asset is considered to be retired when permanently withdrawn from use in a trade or business or in the production of income by the taxpayer.[21] A retirement can occur as the result of a sale or exchange, by any other act of the taxpayer amounting to a permanent disposition of the asset, by physical abandonment of the asset, or by transfer of the asset to supplies or scrap.[22] The retirement rules under facts-and-circumstances depreciation and under the Guideline Class Life System are similar.

If property is both placed in service and "disposed of" (presumably including all retirements except transfers to supplies or scrap) during the taxable year, such property is included in the Class Life ADR election unless one of the optional exclusions is elected.[23] Not all optional exclusions apply for this purpose. The 10-percent used property rule and the exclusion for carryover property do not apply.[24] However, the optional exclusions for old investment credit property,[25] amortization property,[26] buildings,[27] and subsidiary assets[28] are applicable to determine if these assets are included or excluded.

4.4 General Averaging Conventions

Averaging conventions have been in use for more than 45 years,[29] but substantial changes have taken place over the past four years. These changes apply to the Class Life ADR System. This subsection analyzes the prior rules, which are still in effect if Class Life ADR depreciation is not elected.

The general regulations for averaging conventions enumerate three specific conventions, but this list is not exclusive and other conventions may be used.[30]

The first of the enumerated averaging conventions is the half-year convention.[31] The half-year convention treats all acquisitions and retirements as made at the middle of the taxable year, as if the purchases and sales were made uniformly during the year. This convention allows a half-year's depreciation on all acquisitions and retirements during the year. The examples in Tables 8–10 demonstrate the application of the half-year convention to various depreciation methods.

TABLE 8. Half-year convention, straight-line method.

Asset Year	Depreciation	Taxable Year			
		1	2	3	4
1	$1/3$	$1/6$	$1/6$		
2	$1/3$		$1/6$	$1/6$	
3	$1/3$			$1/6$	$1/6$
Total	$3/3$	$1/6$	$2/6$	$2/6$	$1/6$

TABLE 9. Half-year convention, sum of the years-digits.

Asset Year	Depreciation	Taxable Year			
		1	2	3	4
1	$3/6$	$3/12$	$3/12$		
2	$2/6$		$2/12$	$2/12$	
3	$1/6$			$1/12$	$1/12$
Total	$6/6$	$3/12$	$5/12$	$3/12$	$1/12$

The depreciation for an asset that has a 3-year life is $1/3$ per year under the straight-line method. However, each year's depreciation must be split between taxable years, since only half the first year's depreciation is taken for the year of acquisition (Table 9). Salvage value is assumed to be zero in this example.

The annual depreciation charges are allocated in much the same way as straight-line depreciation. Only the declining balance methods are computed differently, as Table 10 shows in the case of double declining balance depreciation and an asset with a 3-year life and no salvage value. Here, the declining balance rate is $2/3$, so the rate for the first year is $1/3$.

Table 10 reflects double declining balance depreciation and assumes that the asset was actually disposed of after 3 years. If the asset had been retained, depreciation would continue, and would be $4/81$ in the fourth year.

The other averaging convention that received widespread application under the general averaging convention rules is the full-year convention.[32] The full-year convention treats all acquisitions and retirements during the first half of the taxable year as made on the first day of the taxable year, and all acquisitions and retirements during the second half of the taxable year as made on the first day of the succeeding taxable year.[33]

When the full-year convention is applied, depreciation for a year is never split up, as it is in the case of the half-year convention (see Tables 8–10). Acquisitions during the first half of the taxable year

TABLE 10. Half-year convention, double declining balance.

Taxable Year	Depreciation
1	$1/3$
2	$(1 - 1/3)\ 2/3 = 4/9$
3	$(1 - 1/3 - 4/9)\ 2/3 = 4/27$
4	$(1 - 1/3 - 4/9 - 4/27)\ 1/3 = 2/81$

receive a full year's depreciation in the year of acquisition, while acquisitions during the second half of the taxable year receive no depreciation until the following year. Retirements during the first half of the taxable year receive no depreciation in the year of retirement, but retirements during the second half of the taxable year receive a full year's depreciation in the year of retirement.[34]

The dividing point between the first half of the taxable year and the second half of the taxable year is normally measured in months, not days. Thus, for a calendar year taxpayer, June 30 marks the end of the first half of the taxable year and July 1 marks the beginning of the second half of the taxable year.

Taxpayers are not limited to the half-year convention or the full-year convention, but may devise other conventions, such as a convention based on months.[35] These other conventions are rarely used, however.

When depreciation is based on facts and circumstances, taxpayers are not required to use an averaging convention. On the other hand, taxpayers are not entitled to the use of an averaging convention as a matter of right. Averaging conventions are available only for multiple asset accounts, not when one-of-a-kind assets are acquired.[36] If an averaging convention is used, it must be consistently followed for the items or account to which it applies, and must be used for both additions and retirements.

The Regulations bar the use of an averaging convention in any year in which it would substantially distort the depreciation allowance for that taxable year. Such distortions occur where a large proportion of a taxpayer's acquisitions are made in the first half of the taxable year and the taxpayer desires to use the full-year convention; or occur where a large proportion of the purchases are made near the close of the taxable year and the taxpayer desires to use the half-year convention.

In a recent ruling, Rev. Rul. 73-202, the use of the half-year convention was barred on the premise that it created such a distortion.[37] In this case, machinery costing $1,600,000 was placed in service on December 20. During the prior 10 years, the cost of machinery purchased during any year did not exceed $250,000 and the machinery was purchased throughout the year. It was anticipated that this earlier pattern would be repeated in later years.[38] The ruling is unsatisfactory in that it does not indicate how much weight is placed on the lateness of the year in which the assets were acquired and how much weight was placed on the large cost of the assets compared with those acquired in prior years.

The Regulations do not refer to distortions in depreciation caused by retirements. Consequently, taxpayers using the full-year convention can maximize depreciation by deferring retirements until after the midpoint of the taxable year, while taxpayers using the half-year convention can maximize depreciation by deferring retirements until just after the beginning of the following taxable year.

Averaging conventions do not require a formal election. In essence, they are elected on the tax return as part of the depreciation computation.

These averaging conventions are applicable to assets not covered by the Class Life ADR depreciation system, because they were acquired previously, because the taxpayer does not elect the Class Life ADR System, or because the assets were excluded from the election.

4.5 A Year of Confusion—1971

In 1970, following the repeal of the investment credit as part of the Tax Reform Act of 1969, the Treasury Department considered various alternatives for liberalization of depreciation. One alternative considered was the full-year convention, used in Canada since 1949, which permits a full year's depreciation in the year of purchase and no depreciation in the year of sale.* In 1971, the Asset Depreciation Range System (ADR) was promulgated. The Canadian type full-year convention was not adopted, but a $3/4$ convention was introduced.†

The ADR system specified three averaging conventions: the half-year convention, the modified half-year convention, and an alternative form of the modified half-year convention.

The half-year convention permitted a taxpayer to treat all additions during the year as having been made in the middle of the year, so that half a year's depreciation could be taken in the year of acquisition.[39] This convention was in use prior to ADR, as we have seen.

The modified half-year convention was, in effect, a $3/4$ convention: The taxpayer could treat all additions during the first half of the taxable year as having been made at the beginning of the year, so that a full year's depreciation could be taken in the year of acquisition. Acquisitions during the second half of the taxable year would be treated as having been made at the middle of the taxable year, so that a half-year's depreciation on these assets could be taken in the year of acquisition.[40]

*Feinschreiber, "Depreciation Reform: Recent Treasury Study Reveals Liberalization Alternatives," *Journal of Taxation,* October 1970; Davis, *Capital Cost Allowance* (Studies of the Royal Commission on Taxation No. 21), 1966, p. 29.

†Sunley, "The 1971 Depreciation Revision: Measures of Effectiveness," 24 *National Tax Journal,* 1971, pp. 19–30.

The alternate form of the modified half-year convention treated all acquisitions during the year as having taken place on the first day of the second quarter of the taxable year, so that $\frac{3}{4}$ of year's depreciation could be taken in the year of acquisition.[41]

The ADR Regulations failed to specify whether the alternate form of the modified half-year convention was a separate convention for consistency purposes.* The Regulations also failed to permit the use of the full-year convention.† This was a serious defect, because the use of an averaging convention was mandatory under ADR,** and that convention has long been in widespread use.

During the consideration of the Revenue Act of 1971, the $\frac{3}{4}$ convention came under increasing attack. It was felt that this convention would provide too great an incentive and too great a revenue loss when combined with the reinstatement of the investment credit.[42] As a result, Congress enacted the following provision as part of the Revenue Act of 1971:

Sec. 167(m)(2)-Certain first-year conventions not permitted. No convention with respect to the time at which assets are deemed placed in service shall be permitted under this section which generally would provide greater depreciation allowances during the taxable year in which the assets are placed in service than would be permitted if all assets were placed in service ratably throughout the year and if depreciation allowances were computed without regard to any convention.

Section 167(m) (2) bars the $\frac{3}{4}$ convention because it would produce more depreciation than if assets were placed in service ratably throughout the year. In other respects, however, the statute is ambiguous. The statute refers to conventions "generally provid(ing) greater depreciation." The final clause, "if depreciation allowances were computed without regard to any convention," could conceivably be interpreted to preclude the use of any convention that is favorable to the taxpayer. The actual interpretation of this clause is that it merely modifies the preceding clause, "if all assets were placed in service ratably throughout the year," so that any convention that produces a half-year's depreciation for assets placed in service during the year would be permitted by statute.

*Feinschreiber, "Treasury Moves to Increase Depreciation," 5 *International Tax Institute Proceedings* 112, 1971.

†Feinschreiber, "New Regulations Liberalize Tax Depreciation," *The New York Certified Public Accountant,* September 1971, p. 638.

**Feinschreiber, "New Regulations Liberalize Tax Depreciation," *The New York Certified Public Accountant,* September 1971, p. 638.

4.6 Averaging Conventions Under the Class Life ADR System

The new depreciation regulations provide two first-year averaging conventions. Taxpayers depreciating assets under the Class Life ADR System must use one of these two conventions.[43] The same convention must be adopted for all assets placed in service during the year, even if the assets are in different classes.[44] However, a different convention may be selected for assets placed in service in a later year.[45] The two conventions are called the "half-year convention" and the "modified half-year convention."

The half-year convention, as under ADR and prior Regulations, treats all acquisitions during the year as being placed in service on the first day of the second half of the taxable year.[46] Thus, all property placed in service during the year receives a half-year's depreciation. For the purposes of computing remaining life, it is assumed that a half-year's depreciation is taken on all assets.[47]

Under the earlier ADR system, the term "modified half-year convention" referred to a $3/4$ convention. Now, under the Class Life ADR System, the term "modified half-year convention" describes a convention similar to the "full-year convention," which has been in widespread use but was banned under ADR as promulgated in 1971 (see *Section 4.5*).

The modified half-year convention treats all property placed in service during the first half of the taxable year as being placed in service on the first day of the taxable year, and all property placed in service during the second half of the taxable year as being placed in service on the first day of the succeeding taxable year.[48] Thus, assets placed in service during the second half of the taxable year will receive no depreciation in that year. In this respect, the modified half-year convention is identical with the full-year convention.

The full-year convention and the modified half-year convention differ in other respects. Where an asset is acquired in the second half of the taxable year, the full-year convention will treat the asset as acquired in the following taxable year in all respects. Under the modified half-year convention, recognition is given to the fact that the asset was acquired in the earlier year, even though no depreciation was taken for the asset during that year. This affects the computation of remaining life, as we shall see in the following paragraph.

Under the full-year convention, assets acquired during the first half of the year are deemed to have received a full-year's depreciation for the purpose of computing the remaining life at the end of the first year. Assets acquired during the second half of the year are deemed to have received no depreciation for purposes of computing the remaining life at the end of the first year. Under the modified half-year convention, all assets are deemed to have received a half-year's depreciation for purposes of the remaining life computation.[49]

A taxpayer can elect the Class Life ADR System and have a choice between the half-year convention and the modified half-year convention only, or can depreciate its assets under the facts-and-circumstances method of determining useful life and choose the half-year convention, the full-year convention, or others. While the suitability of first-year conventions is only one factor in the decision whether the Class Life ADR System should be elected, nevertheless it should be considered.

The new modified half-year convention may produce greater acceleration of depreciation than the full-year convention in use outside the Class Life ADR System, as the following two examples illustrate. In both examples, sum of the years-digits depreciation is used, salvage value is zero, and the taxpayer uses a calendar year for tax purposes.

This first example shows that three assets, each with a useful life of $5\frac{1}{2}$ years, were acquired and placed in service in 1975 as follows:

Asset A	March 15, 1975	$ 40,000
Asset B	June 13, 1975	50,000
Asset C	July 30, 1975	10,000
Total		$100,000

Here we use a $5\frac{1}{2}$-year life so as to follow the proposed regulations from which this example is taken. A fractional life can result from using Class Life ADR.[50,*]

Table 11 compares depreciation under the two conventions.

TABLE 11

Year	Modified Half-Year Convention	Full-Year Convention	Difference
1975	$ 27,500	$ 27,500	0
1976	27,778	25,555	$2,223
1977	22,222	20,000	2,222
1978	16,667	14,445	2,222
1979	5,833	8,889	(3,056)
1980	0	3,333	(3,333)
1981	0	278	(278)
Total	$100,000	$100,000	0

*Feinschreiber, "How New First-Year Convention Under ADR Can Speed Up Depreciation," *The Practical Accountant,* November–December 1972, pp. 39–40; "Computing Depreciation Under the 'Class Life' System," *The CPA Journal,* October 1973, pp. 857–862.

The sum of the years-digits for a $5^1/_2$-year life is 18 ($5^1/_2$, plus $4^1/_2$, plus $3^1/_2$, etc.) so that depreciation fractions will range from $^{5.5}/_{18}$ at the start to $^{0.5}/_{18}$ at the end. Thus, the first-year depreciation in our example is $27,500 ($^{5.5}/_{18}$ times the $90,000 in assets acquired through June 30).

Under the "modified half-year convention," a half-year is deemed to have elapsed in the year of acquisition, not only as to $90,000 but also as to the $10,000 in assets acquired on July 30, 1972. Thus, the second-year depreciation is the remaining half of the $^{5.5}/_{18}$ plus half of $^{4.5}/_{18}$ (averaging out to $^5/_{18}$) on the entire $100,000 in the account. This split computation carries through for the remaining years until 1979, when the full cost will have been recovered.

Under the "full-year convention," it is recognized that a full-year's depreciation was taken in the year of acquisition on the $90,000 of assets and that no depreciation was taken on the $10,000 asset. Thus, separate fractions are used for the $90,000 and the $10,000. In other words, the depreciation computation is the same in 1975, but in 1976 it becomes $(^{4.5}/_{18} \times \$90,000) + (^{5.5}/_{18} \times \$10,000)$.

The second example illustrates a more extreme situation, but one permitted under the Class Life ADR Regulations, in which all assets were acquired during the first half of the taxable year. Two assets, each with a useful life of three years, were acquired and placed in service in 1975 as follows:

Asset X	April 18, 1975	$ 45,000
Asset Y	May 5, 1975	55,000
Total		$100,000

The comparative depreciation under the two conventions would be as follows:

Year	Modified Half-Year Convention	Full-Year Convention	Difference
1975	$ 50,000	$ 50,000	0
1976	41,667	33,333	$8,334
1977	8,333	16,667	(8,334)
Total	$100,000	$100,000	0

On a 3-year life, sum of the years-digits depreciation amounts to $^3/_6$, $^2/_6$, and $^1/_6$, respectively. Thus, depreciation in the first year under both conventions is $50,000 ($^3/_6$ times the cost of assets acquired in the first half of the year; that is, the entire $100,000). Since all assets were acquired before June 30, 1975, maximum depreciation in the year of acquisition is allowed under either convention.

As in the first example, under the "modified half-year convention," only one-half of a year is deemed to have elapsed in the first year (for purposes of future depreciation), so that half of the $3/6$ still remains at the end of the first year. Thus, for the second year, the remaining half of the $3/6$ is utilized together with half of the $2/6$, giving us depreciation of \$41,667 ($5/12$ of \$100,000). For the third year, the remaining half of the $2/6$ is utilized together with half of the $1/6$. For the fourth year, the remaining half of the $1/6$ is applied. (Of course, no depreciation would be allowed after asset cost is recovered.)

Under the "full-year convention" the 1976 percentage is simply $2/6$, giving us depreciation of \$33,333. Only one computation is necessary, since both assets were acquired in the same half of the year.

The modified half-year convention can be disadvantageous for other accounts in which acquisitions take place primarily in the latter half of the taxable year. There, depreciation will be delayed. Unfortunately for taxpayers under the Class Life ADR System, the same convention must be used for all assets acquired during the same taxable year.[51] However, the same convention need not be adopted for assets placed in service in other taxable years.[52]

REFERENCES

1. 10(b), *Kern Co.,* 1 TC 249.
2. 11(e)(1)(i).
3. 11(e)(1)(i).
4. 11(e)(1)(i).
5. Reg. Sec. 1.46-3(d)(1)(ii);
   Reg. Sec. 1.46-3(d)(2).
6. 11(e)(1)(i).
7. 11(e)(1)(i).
8. 11(e)(1)(i).
9. 11(e)(1)(i).
10. 11(e)(1)(i).
11. 11(d)(2).
12. 11(e)(1)(ii).
13. 11(d)(2)(iv)(*a*);11(d)(2)(vii)(*a*);
    11(d)(2)(viii)(*a*).
14. 11(e)(1)(iv).
15. 11(e)(1)(iii)(*a*).
16. 11(e)(1)(iii)(*a*);11(d)(2)(iv)(*b*);
    11(d)(2)(vii)(*b*); 11(d)(2)(viii)(*b*).
17. 11(e)(1)(iii)(*b*).
18. 11(e)(1)(v).
19. 11(c)(2); 11(e)(1)(i).
20. 11(e)(1)(i).
21. 11(d)(3)(i).
22. 11(d)(3)(i).
23. 11(e)(2).
24. 11(b)(5)(iii); 11(b)(7).
25. 11(b)(5)(iv).
26. 11(b)(5)(v).
27. 11(b)(5)(vi).
28. 11(b)(5)(vii).
29. *Hillyer, Deutsch, Edwards, Inc.*
    21 BTA 452; *Scovill Mfg. Co.*
    25 BTA 265; *Clark Thread Co.*
    100 F.2d 257; *Spang-Chal-
    font & Co. Inc.* 9 BTA 858;
    Benham Ice Cream Co. 5
    BTA 97; *Hyam's Coal Co.* 1
    BTA 217.
30. 10(b).
31. 10(b).
32. 10(b).
33. 10(b).
34. 10(b).
35. CCH Standard Federal Tax
    Reports Par. 1732.20.
36. 10(b).
37. 1973–18 I.R.B. 32.
38. Rev. Rul. 73–202, 1973–18
    I.R.B. 32.

39. 11(c)(2)(iii).
40. 11(c)(2)(ii).
41. 11(c)(2)(ii).
42. Report of the Senate
Committee on
Finance to Accompany H.R.
10947 (1971).
43. 11(c)(2)(i).
44. 11(c)(2)(i).

45. 11(c)(2)(i).
46. 11(c)(2)(iii).
47. 11(c)(1)(iii)(*d*).
48. 11(c)(1)(ii).
49. 11(c)(1)(ii).
50. 11(c)(1)(iii)(*f*).
51. 11(c)(2)(i).
52. 11(c)(2)(i).

5

Salvage Value

5.1 Introduction to Salvage Value

"Salvage value" is a term and concept that has gradually become well defined in the tax law, though determination of salvage value in specific instances continues to present practical problems. This chapter focuses on the general features of salvage value, then on the special salvage value rules under the Class Life ADR System and the Guideline Class Life System, and finally on the factual determinations of salvage value and the impact of salvage value on depreciation computations.

5.2 Fundamental Aspects of Salvage Value

Salvage value is the amount estimated to be realizable upon sale or other disposition of an asset when it is retired from service by a taxpayer at the time it is no longer useful in the taxpayer's trade or business or in the production of the taxpayer's income.[1] Salvage value is generally determined as of the time of acquisition,[2] though a somewhat different rule applies when Class Life ADR depreciation is elected[3] (see *Section 5.4*).

The Regulations state that salvage value is not changed at any time after it is determined, merely because of changes in price levels.[4] Because inflation has persisted at a high rate during the past decade, this provision is particularly important. Actual proceeds from the retirement of an asset may exceed estimated salvage by a wide margin

55

because of inflation. Even if expected proceeds increase because of inflation during the life of an asset, estimated salvage value will not be changed. Consequently, annual depreciation charges will not be reduced because of inflation.

If the Class Life ADR depreciation system or the Guideline Class Life System is not elected, the Internal Revenue Service has the power to redetermine useful life.[5] If useful life is redetermined, salvage value may also be determined, based upon the facts known at the time of such redetermination of useful life.[6] Because of the high level of continuing inflation and its effect on actual proceeds, the Class Life ADR System and the Guideline Class Life System produce a significant advantage from the standpoint of salvage value: The Internal Revenue Service is unable to redetermine useful life and therefore loses this opportunity to increase salvage value.

Salvage value and useful life interrelate in one other important respect. If the taxpayer's policy is to dispose of assets that are still in good operating condition, the salvage may represent a relatively large proportion of the original basis of the asset.[7] A number of cases concerning automobiles illustrate this principle. Where rental cars and other automobiles are used for periods comparatively shorter than the physical life of these assets, salvage value is not junk value but is the resale value at the time of disposal by the taxpayer.[8] Thus, in cases where rental automobiles were used for 18 months, salvage value was 60 percent of cost.[9]

On the other hand, if the taxpayer customarily uses an asset until its inherent useful life has been substantially exhausted, salvage value may represent no more than junk value.[10] A ruling indicates that junk or scrap value may be used only where the taxpayer follows the practice of using depreciable property for its full service life.[11]

The presence of salvage value may or may not affect annual depreciation charges, depending on the depreciation method utilized and whether or not Class Life ADR depreciation is elected (see Section 5.8). This salvage value limitation does not apply to the 20-percent additional first-year depreciation.[12] However, in no event can an asset be depreciated below a reasonable salvage value.[13] If assets are placed in a multiple-asset account, the account cannot be depreciated below its reasonable salvage value.[14]

The one basic rule for salvage value that pervades all others, regardless of the use of Class Life depreciation or facts-and-circumstances depreciation, and regardless of the depreciation method used, is that salvage value limits allowable depreciation.[15] Salvage value limits depreciation by placing a floor on the adjusted basis of an asset or account. An asset or account can be depreciated from its cost or other initial basis down to a point where salvage value equals the adjusted basis. This limitation can also be viewed as restricting the total depreciation to an amount equal to original basis minus salvage value.

EXAMPLE 1

Original basis	$10,000
Less depreciation taken	7,000
Less salvage value	1,000
Remaining available depreciation	$ 2,000

EXAMPLE 2

Original basis	$8,000
Salvage value	3,000
Allowable depreciation	$5,000

5.3 Gross Versus Net Salvage Value

Gross salvage value is, in general, the amount that will be realized on disposition of an asset at the end of its useful life without taking any offsets into account. Net salvage value is gross salvage value less the cost of removal, dismantling, demolition, or similar operations.[16] This is the definition of net salvage value in the Class Life ADR depreciation regulations. The Guideline Class Life depreciation system also uses these definitions of "gross salvage" and "net salvage."[17] However, the general depreciation regulations applicable to facts-and-circumstances depreciation define "net salvage" value as gross salvage less costs of removal.[18] These particular regulations contain no reference costs of dismantling, demolition, or similar operations.

When depreciation is based on facts and circumstances, either gross or net salvage value can be used, but the practice for treating salvage value must be consistently followed and the treatment of the costs of removal must be consistent with the practice adopted.[19] Almost invariably, net salvage value is used because it produces a lower salvage value amount. If depreciation is computed under the Class Life ADR System, net salvage value is prohibited and gross salvage value must be used.[20] If depreciation is computed under the Guidelines Class Life System, either gross or net salvage may be used.[21] Net salvage is generally used because it is a smaller amount.

Although the Class Life ADR System requires gross salvage value to be used, some of the advantages of net salvage value are in essence obtainable by considering salvage proceeds as net of removal costs. This could be accomplished by selling the retired assets at plant site and having the purchaser responsible for dismantling and removal.

5.4 The Timing of Salvage Value Determination

The time at which salvage value is determined has an important bearing on the internal corporate methods for determining salvage value and even upon the amount of salvage value determined. Because inflation tends to increase the residual value of an asset, salvage value is likely to be higher if it is ascertained at a later point in time.

If depreciation is based on facts and circumstances, salvage value is theoretically determined at the time of asset acquisition.[22] As a practical matter, salvage value is usually determined prior to acquisition or subsequent to acquisition, but should be based on data as of the time of acquisition.

If the Class Life ADR depreciation system is utilized, salvage value must be estimated at the time the Class Life ADR election is made, and must be based upon the facts and circumstances existing at the close of the taxable year in which the asset is placed in service.[23]

Thus, under facts-and-circumstances depreciation, salvage value must be determined on an asset-by-asset basis as each asset is acquired. In contrast, salvage value under the Class Life ADR depreciation system must be determined at one time for all assets placed in service during the taxable year. The Class Life ADR rule is easier to apply, but might result in higher salvage values because the determination is made at a later time.

For example, in the case of a calendar-year taxpayer using the Class Life ADR System, if an asset is acquired and placed in service on November 16, 1974, salvage value is determined as of December 31, 1974, and the actual determination may be made as late as September 15, 1975, 8½ months after the close of the taxable year (assuming the return is timely filed, including extensions to file). Under facts-and-circumstances depreciation, salvage value would theoretically be determined on November 16, 1974.

If, in the preceding example, the asset acquired on November 16, 1974, were not placed in service until February 1, 1975, salvage value under the Class Life ADR System would be determined as of December 31, 1975, and the actual determination could be made as late as September 15, 1976 (assuming the return is timely filed, including extensions to file). Under facts-and-circumstances depreciation, salvage value would still be determined as of November 16, 1974.

If the Guideline Class Life depreciation system is used, one date is used for the determination of salvage value, since Guideline Class Life depreciation applies only to assets already owned by the taxpayer. For details, see *Section 5.7.*

5.5 Salvage Value Reduction for Personal Property

A statutory provision allows a reduction in salvage value for personal property. Eligible property includes desks, lathes, stamping presses, and patents, but not office buildings, land, cattle, or mink. This reduction is generally utilized when available because most taxpayers seek to minimize salvage value and increase tax depreciation.

This provision enables salvage value to be reduced by as much as 10 percent of an asset's basis.[24] Thus, if salvage value before the reduction is no more than 10 percent of basis, salvage value can then be ignored entirely. Consider the following examples:

EXAMPLE 1

Asset basis	$2,000
Salvage value before reduction	300
Salvage value reduction	200
Salvage value after reduction	100
Amount depreciable	$1,900

EXAMPLE 2

Asset basis	$7,000
Salvage value before reduction	500
Salvage value reduction	500
Salvage value after reduction	0
Amount depreciable	$7,000

This salvage value reduction applies under facts-and-circumstances depreciation, Class Life ADR depreciation, and Guideline Class Life depreciation.

Not all property qualifies for this salvage value reduction. Only depreciable personal property other than livestock is eligible,[25] but the items can be tangible[26] or intangible.[27] Additionally, the personal property must have a useful life of 3 years or more, determined as of the time of acquisition.[28] Used assets as well as new are eligible.[29]

The ceiling on the salvage value reduction of 10 percent of basis is computed as of the time at which salvage value is required to be determined, or is redetermined.[30] The salvage value reduction can be used for some assets, but not others, at the option of the taxpayer.[31] Consistency is not required.

There are no dollar limits on the salvage value reduction, unlike the additional first-year depreciation under Section 179. Consequently, there is no need to select from among eligible assets. Usually, the salvage value reduction is applied to all eligible assets.

The salvage reduction affects tax depreciation in two ways. First, in situations in which salvage value affects annual depreciation charges, the reduction in salvage value will provide greater depreciation each year. Second, the reduction in salvage value affects the ceiling on depreciation, which is the undepreciable portion of an account. An asset or an account may not be depreciated below salvage value, but for this purpose the salvage value is determined after taking into account the Section 167(f) reduction.[32]

One problem area in applying the Section 167(f) salvage value reduction is the delineation of "tangible personal property." "Tangible personal property," for purposes of the salvage value reduction, has the same meaning as in the case of qualification for the investment tax credit.[33] Consequently, the salvage value reduction is not affected by the categorization of assets under state law as personal property or as fixtures. However, other tangible property used as an integral part of a qualified activity (such as manufacturing, production, extraction, or public utility service), but not constituting tangible personal property, will not qualify for the salvage value reduction.

The delineation of intangible personal property presents a different type of problem. Many intangibles such as goodwill and certain customer lists have been held not to be depreciable. Consequently, the threshold question to be answered before computing the salvage value reduction is whether the intangible asset is depreciable.

This Regulation contains detailed provisions for determining when an asset is acquired. The purpose of this rule is to establish a cutoff date so that the salvage value reduction will apply only to assets acquired after October 16, 1962. This cutoff date is not of importance for currently acquired assets, but it does affect the current depreciation of assets acquired on or before October 1962, as well as the salvage value ceiling on allowable depreciation for those assets. For this reason, and because acquisition dates play an important role in other aspects of tax depreciation, these rules merit our present attention.

Property is deemed to be acquired when reduced to physical possession or control.[34] Property not previously used in the taxpayer's trade or business or held for the production of income and converted to such use is deemed to be acquired on the date of such conversion.[35]

The redetermination of salvage value at the time useful life is redetermined (if such redetermination results under facts-and-circumstances depreciation) causes some complexities from the standpoint of the Section 167(f) salvage value reduction. The salvage value reduction is based on the purchase price, not on the unrecovered basis.[36] Consequently, the salvage value reduction may offset, at least in part, the increase in salvage value at the time useful life is redetermined. This rule applies even when the redeterminations are precipitated by the taxpayer's change in depreciation method.[37]

For purposes of the three-year minimum life for applying the Section 167(f) salvage value reduction, it is unclear whether actual useful life is to be used or asset life is to be based on applicable guidelines or asset depreciation ranges. It appears that actual useful life is to be applied, however.

The livestock exclusion applies to horses, cattle, hogs, sheep, goats, mink, and other fur-bearing animals, irrespective of the use to which they are put or the purpose for which they are held.[38]

A planning opportunity that is not specified in the regulations, but which appears to be valid, is the application of the Section 167(f) salvage value deduction on a group basis rather than on an asset-by-asset basis. Refer to Examples 1 and 2 of salvage value reduction given at the beginning of this section. If the assets are combined, the salvage value reduction is greater, as the illustration below indicates.

	Example 1	Example 2	Combined
Asset basis	$2,000	$7,000	$9,000
Salvage value before reduction	300	500	800
Salvage value reduction	200	500	800
Salvage value after reduction	100	0	0
Amount depreciable	$1,900	$7,000	$9,000

The Section 167(f) salvage value reduction should be used when it applies unless the taxpayer desires to minimize depreciation.

5.6 Salvage Value Under the Class Life ADR System

The Class Life ADR salvage value rules generally follow the salvage value rules established for facts-and-circumstances depreciation. These rules are described in this section, and differences from the facts-and-circumstances treatment of salvage value are highlighted.

Salvage value is determined for each vintage account.[39] Vintage accounts usually are multiple-asset accounts, so the determination of salvage value on an asset-by-asset basis is not necessary. Salvage value may be reduced by up to 10 percent of the asset's basis.[40] See Section 5.5 for the details of this salvage value reduction. The estimated salvage value before this reduction must be affirmatively ascertained, so the taxpayer must maintain records reasonably sufficient to determine the facts and circumstances taken into account in estimating salvage value.[41]

Many tax professionals view the Class Life ADR System as prohibiting all IRS adjustments to salvage value once the salvage value is ascertained. However, the actual provision in the regulations contains a somewhat less extensive prohibition on adjustments by the IRS: "The salvage value estimated by the taxpayer will not be redetermined merely as a result of fluctuations in price levels or as a result of other facts and circumstances occurring after the close of the taxable year of elections."[42]

Under the Class Life ADR System, salvage value means gross salvage, so no reduction for the cost of removal, dismantling, demolition, or similar operations may be made.[43] Gross salvage is the amount that (it is estimated) will be realized upon a sale or other disposition of the property in a vintage account when it is no longer useful in the taxpayer's trade or business or production of income and is retired from service.[44] These Regulations also include the familiar rule that gross salvage value may constitute a relatively large proportion of the unadjusted basis (usually cost) of an asset if the asset is customarily sold when it is relatively new and in good operating condition.[45] Gross salvage value is the amount expected to be realized upon such sale or other disposition.[46] See *Section 5.3* for details concerning gross salvage value.

As is the usual case, salvage value under the Class Life ADR System limits allowable depreciation. In no case may a vintage account be depreciated below a reasonable salvage value after taking into account any reduction in gross salvage value permitted by Section 167(f).[47] However, salvage value does not affect annual depreciation allowances, regardless of the depreciation method or methods used.[48]

When the repair allowance (see Chapter 6) is elected, and eligible expenditures exceed the repair allowance percentage, the excess is capitalized as a "property improvement."[49] However, salvage value for an account need not be established or increased as the result of such a property improvement.[50]

5.6.1 Limits on Salvage Value Adjustments by IRS

The Class Life ADR System contains a special rule that limits salvage value adjustments by the Internal Revenue Service. The theoretical underpinning for this rule is that the salvage value established by a taxpayer for a vintage account will not be redetermined if it is reasonable.[51] Further, since the determination of salvage value is a matter of estimation, minimal adjustments will not be made.[52] Consequently, the salvage value established by the taxpayer will be deemed reasonable unless there is sufficient basis in facts and circumstances (existing at the close of the taxable year) for a significant redetermination of salvage value.[53]

For a redetermination of salvage value to be made, the IRS must determine for the account a salvage value that exceeds the salvage value established by the taxpayer for the account.[54] Further, this excess must be greater than 10 percent of the unadjusted basis of the account at the close of the taxable year in which the account is established.[55] This particular rule is sometimes erroneously conceived as providing an extra 10-percent salvage value reduction. Some taxpayers falsely assume that where salvage value is actually 20 percent, they can use a 10-percent salvage value figure and then reduce this amount to zero by virtue of Section 167(f). The Regulations provide that this salvage value leeway rule will not apply in situations where the taxpayer follows the practice of understating estimates of gross salvage value to take advantage of this provision.[56]

If salvage value is adjusted, the adjustment is made by increasing the salvage value by the difference between the actual determination of salvage value and the amount previously determined by the taxpayer.[57] For this purpose, a determination of salvage value can be made on audit, through appellate proceedings, or otherwise, including a "final determination."[58] This salvage value adjustment rule also applies when depreciation is based on the Guideline Class Life System.[59]

The Regulations provide four examples of the application of the limitation on adjustment of salvage value. In the first example, there are two assets in the vintage account, and both qualify for the salvage value adjustment of Section 167(f).[60] Ten percent of the taxpayer's unadjusted basis is $8,000. This exceeds the proposed adjustment of $5,000 ($52,000 − $47,000) so no adjustment will be made.

EXAMPLE 1

	Taxpayer's Computation	IRS Computation
Unadjusted basis, asset Y	$50,000	$50,000
Unadjusted basis, asset Z	30,000	30,000
Total unadjusted basis	80,000	80,000
Total gross salvage value	55,000	60,000
Reduction in salvage value	8,000	8,000
Salvage value	$47,000	$52,000

In the second example, the facts are the same as in the first except that the taxpayer's estimated gross salvage value is $50,000.[61] Ten percent of the unadjusted basis is $8,000. The proposed adjustment of

$10,000 ($52,000 − $42,000) exceeds this leeway, so salvage value is adjusted on audit to $52,000.

EXAMPLE 2

	Taxpayer's Computation	IRS Computation
Unadjusted basis	$80,000	$80,000
Gross salvage value	50,000	60,000
Reduction in salvage value	8,000	8,000
Salvage value	$42,000	$52,000

In the third example, the facts are the same as in the first example except that the examining IRS agent determines salvage value to be $66,000 and the appellate conferee then determines salvage value to be $63,000.[62] Ten percent of the unadjusted basis is $8,000. Since the IRS agent determined that salvage value was understated by more than $8,000 ($58,000 − $47,000 = $11,000), salvage value would be readjusted to $58,000. However, the determination by the appellate conferee that salvage value is $55,000 [after Section 167(f) adjustment] makes the proposed adjustment of $8,000 ($55,000 − $47,000) within the $8,000 limit, so no adjustment is made.

EXAMPLE 3

	Taxpayer's Computation	IRS Agent's Computation	Appellate Conferee's Computation
Unadjusted basis	$80,000	$80,000	$80,000
Gross salvage value	55,000	66,000	63,000
Reduction in salvage value	8,000	8,000	8,000
Salvage value	$47,000	$58,000	$55,000

In the fourth example, the account consists of a building that is ineligible for the Section 167(f) salvage value reduction.[63] Ten percent of the unadjusted basis is $9,000. Since the proposed adjustment of $8,000 ($18,000 − $10,000) is less, no adjustment will be made.

EXAMPLE 4

	Taxpayer's Computation	IRS Agent's Computation
Unadjusted basis	$90,000	$90,000
Gross salvage value	$10,000	$18,000

5.6.2 Salvage Value Reductions

Under the Class Life ADR System, salvage value is affected by asset retirements. First, there is a mandatory salvage value reduction when excess proceeds are added to the reserve. Thus, to the extent that accumulated depreciation plus proceeds (together called the "reserve") exceed the unadjusted basis (usually cost) less salvage value, salvage value will be reduced, but not below zero, retroactive to the beginning of the taxable year.[64] For example, if the unadjusted basis of an account is $1,000 and salvage value is $100, salvage value will be reduced to the extent that proceeds from ordinary retirements increase the reserve above $900.[65]

There are also optional salvage value reduction alternatives available to taxpayers, consisting of three basic strategies:

1. As retirements occur, the salvage value of a vintage account may be reduced by the salvage value attributable to the retired asset.[66]

2. As extraordinary but not ordinary retirements occur, salvage value of a vintage account may be reduced by the salvage value attributable to the retired asset.[67]

3. No salvage value adjustments are made.[68]

If salvage value reductions are made, the determination of salvage value attributable to retired assets becomes important. The portion of the salvage value attributable to a retired asset may be determined by multiplying the salvage value for the account by the ratio of the unadjusted basis of the retired asset to the unadjusted basis of the account.[69] This method is not mandatory, so other methods can be used, but the method selected must be consistently applied.[70]

Another, more complicated, salvage value reduction rule is applicable to ordinary retirements only. This particular rule differentiates between retirements by transfer to supplies or scrap and other retirements. When retirements are made other than by transfers to supplies or scrap, salvage value for the account is reduced by the amount of salvage value attributable to the retired asset.[71] This amount is not treated as proceeds, and is therefore not added to the reserve.[72]

In the case of retirements by transfer to supplies or scrap, a taxpayer may reduce salvage value for the account by the amount of salvage value attributable to the retired asset.[73] This amount may or may not be treated as proceeds and added to the reserve. If this amount is not added to the reserve, the basis of the asset in the supplies or scrap account is zero.[74] On the other hand, if this amount is added to the reserve, the asset then acquires this amount as a basis in the supplies or scrap account.[75] However, the amount added to the reserve cannot cause the reserve to exceed the unadjusted basis of the account.[76] The basis of the asset in the supplies or scrap account is the amount actually added to the reserve.[77]

The following three types of removal of an asset from a vintage account are not truly retirements, but nevertheless they permit the salvage value of the account to be reduced by the salvage value attributable to the asset removed:[78]

1. When depreciation of Section 1250 property must be changed pursuant to Section 167(j), the asset must be removed from the vintage account.[79]

2. If property is amortized under one of the special amortization provisions [Sections 167(k), 169, 184, 185, or 187], the property must be removed from the vintage account.[80]

3. If utility depreciation must be normalized, but normalization does not take place, the Class Life ADR System ceases to apply to this property, and the property must be removed from the vintage account.[81]

If salvage value is not reduced as ordinary retirements occur, a taxpayer may nevertheless reduce salvage value when ordinary retirements cause assets to be transferred to supplies or scrap.[82] The basis of the asset in the supplies or scrap account is determined in the following manner: Any reasonable method, such as average cost, conditioned cost, or fair market value, may be consistently applied to value the asset if adequately identified in the taxpayer's books and records.[83] Also, the value of the asset as thus determined cannot exceed its unadjusted basis.[84] The value thus determined is then subtracted from the salvage value for the account, but the salvage value of the account cannot be reduced below zero.[85] The amount by which salvage value is reduced or the value of the asset, whichever is greater, is then treated as proceeds and added to the reserve for the account.[86] The amount added to the reserve then becomes the basis for the retired asset in the supplies or scrap account.[87]

If the adjustments described in the preceding paragraph are made to salvage value, in the case of retirements, by transfer to supplies or scrap, gain will be recognized to the extent that the reserve exceeds the unadjusted basis of the account.[88]

5.7 Salvage Value Under the Guideline Class Life System

The salvage value rules under the Guideline Class Life System follow either the salvage value rules for facts-and-circumstances depreciation (see *Section 5.2*) or the salvage value rules for the Class Life ADR System (see *Section 5.6*), with a few limited exceptions. Although the general approach of this section is to mention all salvage value rules applicable to the Guideline Class Life System, it will concentrate on those rules that are unique to this system.

The Regulations define both gross salvage value and net salvage value, indicating that net salvage value reflects the costs of removal, dismantling, demolition, or similar operations (see *Section 5.3*).[89] A taxpayer may use either gross or net salvage value.[90] The salvage value (whether gross or net) may be reduced by up to 10 percent of basis, pursuant to Section 167(f) (see *Section 5.5*).[91] The Regulations also indicate that salvage value may be a relatively large proportion of unadjusted basis for property sold or otherwise disposed of while relatively new and in good operating condition (see *Section 5.2*).[92]

The annual depreciation allowance is determined without regard to salvage value, similar to Class Life ADR depreciation.[93] However, no account may be depreciated below a reasonable salvage value for the account after the Section 167(f) salvage value reduction.[94] There is a special 10-percent leeway rule for salvage value estimates, so that if the salvage value determined by the IRS does not exceed the salvage value determined by the taxpayer by more than 10 percent of the unadjusted basis of the account, no adjustment will be made (see *Section 5.6.1*).[95]

If a taxpayer had previously been using the Guidelines established by Rev. Proc. 62-21, the establishment of salvage value for years ending in 1971 or afterward will not affect depreciation for prior years.[96]

For the first taxable year for which Guideline Class Life depreciation is elected, the taxpayer must establish salvage value for all qualified property to which the election applies.[97] The aggregate salvage value for each such account must be established.[98] These rules do not constitute permission to change methods of estimating salvage value.[99]

Salvage value will be reduced as retirements occur, but detailed rules are not provided.[100] Salvage value will not be redetermined merely as a result of fluctuations in price levels or other circumstances occurring after the close of the taxable year[101] (see *Section 5.2*). The taxpayer must maintain records reasonably sufficient to identify the salvage value established for each depreciation account.[102]

5.8 Effects of Salvage Value on Depreciation

Salvage value always limits total depreciation because an asset may not be depreciated below salvage value. However, salvage value may also reduce annual depreciation charges in certain instances. In such a case, salvage value is taken into account in advance and each year's depreciation is reduced proportionately. For example: Asset A and asset B each have a 3-year life. After taking the maximum salvage value reduction, asset A has no salvage value but asset B has a salvage value equal to one-third of its cost. The following illustration, using straight-line depreciation, shows the effect of salvage value on each year's depreciation when Class Life depreciation is not elected.*

	Asset A	Asset B
Cost	$9,000	$9,000
Salvage value (after reduction)	0	3,000
Amount depreciable	9,000	6,000
Depreciation year 1	3,000	2,000
Depreciation year 2	3,000	2,000
Depreciation year 3	3,000	2,000
Total depreciation	$9,000	$6,000

Salvage value reduces annual depreciation charges only for certain methods and certain depreciation systems, as the following tabulation indicates by responses to the question: Are annual depreciation charges reduced for salvage value?

	Facts and Circumstances	Class Life ADR[105]	Guideline Class Life[106]
Straight-line depreciation	Yes[103]	No	No
Declining balance methods	No[104]	No	No
Sum of the years-digits	Yes[103]	No	No

Salvage value has a significant impact on selection of the depreciation method when depreciation is based on facts and circumstances, but not when the Class Life ADR System or the Guideline Class Life System is used. Under the Class Life systems, salvage value is never taken into account in *annual* depreciation computations, regardless of the depreciation method used (straight line, declining balance, or sum of the years-digits), so salvage value cannot affect depreciation method selection.

When depreciation is based on facts and circumstances, salvage value affects annual depreciation changes for straight-line depreciation and sum of the years-digits depreciation, but not those for declining balance depreciation. Consequently, when salvage value is high, straight-line depreciation and sum of the years-digits depreciation are substantially reduced throughout the life of asset, but declining balance depreciation is reduced only at the end of the asset's life.

*Feinschreiber, "How Salvage Value Affects Depreciation," *Prentice-Hall Tax Ideas,* Parag. 25,005.

Assuming that an automobile costs $3,000 and has a $1,000 salvage value [after application of Section 167(f)], and that the full-year averaging convention (see Chapter 4) is used,* the comparative effects of the three methods can be tabulated as follows:

Year	Straight Line	Sum of the Years-Digits	Double Declining Balance
1	$ 667	$1,000	$2,000
2	667	667	0
3	666	333	0
Total	$2,000	$2,000	$2,000

Thus, when salvage value is high and depreciation is based on facts and circumstances, the declining balance method tends to be preferable.

5.9 Ascertaining Salvage Value

Salvage value is one of the most difficult amounts to determine, yet salvage value must be ascertained for facts-and-circumstances depreciation, Class Life ADR depreciation, and Guideline Class Life depreciation.

As an asset ages and its productive life expires, its potential proceeds decline (except for the effects of inflation). Consequently, the expected time of disposition is a crucial factor in estimating salvage value. It is important to note that the actual disposition period must be used, not the shorter depreciation period that might be applicable if the Class Life ADR System or the Guideline Class Life System is used, as the following example indicates:

Minimum in ADR range	8
Guideline Life	10
Maximum in ADR range	12
Actual useful life	15

Depreciation may be based on an 8-year life, but salvage value is based on a 15-year life and will therefore be smaller than if it were based on the 8-year life.

The use of empirical data to determine salvage value is often a difficult undertaking, uncertain of success. The leading case in the depreciation field, *Fribourg Navigation*,[107] dealt with depreciation in the year of sale. The case arose because of dramatic changes in actual

*Feinschreiber, "From the Thoughtful Tax Man," *Taxes—The Tax Magazine,* November 1973, pp. 680–682.

salvage value. It is even more difficult to determine salvage value than it is to determine useful life because price-level changes have a significant impact on empirical salvage value data.

A widely applied source of salvage value data is catalog prices for used assets. However, even when such prices are readily available, there are three drawbacks to use of this source from the standpoint of developing salvage value estimates:

1. Assets presently being acquired, for which the salvage value estimates must be developed, are frequently substantially different from assets now being retired and listed in such catalogs.

2. Catalog prices are higher than salvage value estimates should have been for the retired assets because the salvage value estimates should not reflect price-level changes that catalog prices normally reflect.

3. Catalog data is difficult to correlate with a taxpayer's asset-life experience.

Another approach to ascertaining salvage value is to utilize engineering data or other information to compute scrap or junk value. The advantage of this approach is that scrap or junk value for a new asset is readily ascertainable and is likely to produce a low salvage value estimate. When a taxpayer disposes of assets still in operating condition, it may be possible to extrapolate from this scrap or junk value data to arrive at a disposition price. For example, a taxpayer's asset disposition policy may be viewed as a policy of selling assets at a multiple of junk value. The following example illustrates this approach.

Cost	$10,000
Scrap value	300
Multiple	3
Unadjusted salvage value	900
Section 167(f) reduction	900
Salvage value	0

Because of the difficulties in estimating salvage value, some taxpayers attempt to ignore the issue and treat salvage value as zero. Such a taxpayer is in a worse situation than a taxpayer who makes a good-faith determination of salvage value. If a taxpayer does not determine salvage value and prepare supporting documentation and other supporting data, the Internal Revenue Service may have free rein in adjusting salvage value upward.

The risk of IRS salvage value adjustments is quite real. You may recall that in the provisions dealing with limitations on salvage value adjustments, the salvage values for an $80,000 account were $60,000, $58,000, and $66,000.[108] In at least two cases, the courts[109] found salvage value to be at least as high as 60 percent.* Consequently, determination of salvage value merits careful attention.

REFERENCES

1. 1(c)(1), 11(d)(1)(i), 12(c)(1)(i).
2. 1(c)(1).
3. 11(d)(1)(iii).
4. 1(c)(1); *Riss & Co., Inc.*, 28 TCM 1113, Dec. 26,881(M), TC Memo. 1964-190, aff'd, rev'd, and rem'd on other issues (CA-8) 374 F.2d 161, 67-1 USTC 9292; 374 F.2d 173, 67-1 USTC 9293.
5. 1(b).
6. 1(c)(1).
7. 1(c)(1), 11(d)(1)(i), 12(c)(1)(i).
8. *Massey Motors, Inc.* (Supreme Court), 364 U.S. 92, 60-2 USTC 9554; *R. H. Evans* (Supreme Court), 364 U.S. 92, 60-2 USTC 9554, rehearing denied; *Hertz Corp.* (Supreme Court), 364 U.S. 122, 60-2 USTC 9555; *Lynch-Davidson Motors, Inc.* (CA-5) 61-1 USTC 9379.
9. *J. W. Roddy* 20 TCM 1129, Dec. 24,978(M), TC Memo 1961-228.
10. 1(c)(1).
11. Special Ruling, May 18, 1955, CCH '54 Code Transfer Binder 37,233.
12. Reg. Sec. 1.179-1.
13. 1(c)(1), 11(c)(1)(iv), 12(c)(2)(ii).
14. 1(c)(1).
15. Reg. Sec. 1.167(b)-0(a).
16. 11(d)(1)(i).
17. 12(c)(1)(i).
18. 1(c)(1).
19. 1(c)(1).
20. 11(d)(1)(i).
21. 12(c)(1)(i).
22. 1(c)(1).
23. 11(d)(1)(iii).
24. Sec. 167(f).
25. Reg. Sec. 1.167(f)-1(a).
26. Reg. Sec. 1.167(f)-1(b)(1)(i).
27. Reg. Sec. 1.167(f)-1(b)(1)(ii).
28. Reg. Sec. 1.167(f)-1(b)(1).
29. Reg. Sec. 1.167(f)-1(b)(1).
30. Reg. Sec. 1.167(f)-1(a).
31. Reg. Sec. 1.167(f)-1(a).
32. Reg. Sec. 1.167(f)-1(a).
33. Sec. 48(a)(1)(A).
34. Reg. Sec. 1.167(f)-1(b)(2).
35. Reg. Sec. 1.167(f)-1(b)(2).
36. Reg. Sec. 1.167(f)-1(c), Example (2).
37. Reg. Sec. 1.167(f)-1(c), Example (6).
38. Reg. Sec. 1.167(f)-1(b)(1).
39. 11(d)(1)(iii).
40. 11(d)(1)(ii), 11(d)(1)(iii).
41. 11(f)(2)(v), 11(d)(1)(iii).
42. 11(d)(1)(iii).
43. 11(d)(1)(i), 11(d)(1)(ii).
44. 11(d)(1)(i).
45. 11(d)(1)(i).
46. 11(d)(1)(i).
47. 11(d)(1)(iv).
48. 11(c)(1)(i)(*a*).
49. 11(d)(2)(vii).
50. 11(d)(1)(iii).
51. 11(d)(1)(v).
52. 11(d)(1)(v).
53. 11(d)(1)(v).
54. 11(d)(1)(v).
55. 11(d)(1)(v).
56. 11(d)(1)(v).
57. 11(d)(1)(v).
58. Sec. 1313(a)(1), 11(d)(1)(v).
59. 12(c)(3).
60. 11(d)(1)(vi), Example (1).
61. 11(d)(1)(vi), Example (2).
62. 11(d)(1)(vi), Example (3).
63. 11(d)(1)(vi), Example (4).
64. 11(d)(3)(iii).
65. 11(d)(3)(iii).
66. 11(d)(3)(vii)(*b*).
67. 11(d)(3)(vii)(*b*).
68. 11(d)(3)(vii)(*a*).
69. 11(d)(3)(vii)(*c*).

*Feinschreiber, "The Impact of High Salvage Value on Double Declining Balance Depreciation," 20 *South Carolina Law Review* 47 (1968).

70. 11(d)(3)(vii)(*c*).
71. 11(d)(3)(vii)(*d*)(*1*).
72. 11(d)(3)(vii)(*d*)(*1*).
73. 11(d)(3)(vii)(*d*)(*2*).
74. 11(d)(3)(vii)(*d*)(*2*).
75. 11(d)(3)(vii)(*d*)(*2*).
76. 11(d)(3)(vii)(*d*)(*2*).
77. 11(d)(3)(vii)(*d*)(*2*).
78. 11(d)(3)(vii)(*e*).
79. 11(b)(4)(iii).
80. 11(b)(5)(v)(*b*).
81. 11(b)(6)(iii).
82. 11(d)(3)(viii).
83. 11(d)(3)(viii)(*a*).
84. 11(d)(3)(viii)(*a*).
85. 11(d)(3)(viii)(*b*).
86. 11(d)(3)(viii)(*b*).
87. 11(d)(3)(viii)(*c*).
88. 11(d)(3)(viii).
89. 12(c)(1)(i).
90. 12(c)(1)(ii).
91. 12(c)(1)(ii).
92. 12(c)(1)(i).
93. 12(a)(5)(vi).
94. 12(a)(5)(vi), 12(c)(2)(ii).
95. 12(c)(3).
96. 12(c)(2)(iii).
97. 12(c)(2)(i).
98. 12(e)(3)(iv)(*c*).
99. 12(c)(2)(i).
100. 12(c)(2)(i).
101. 12(c)(2)(i).
102. 12(c)(2)(i).
103. 1(c)(1).
104. Reg. Sec. 1.167(b)-1, Reg. Sec. 1.167(b)-2, Reg. Sec. 1.167(b)-3.
105. 11(c)(1)(i)(*a*).
106. 12(a)(5)(vi).
107. 383 U.S. 272, 86 S.C.T. 862, 66-1 USTC 9280.
108. 11(d)(1)(v), 12(c)(4).
109. *J. W. Roddy,* 20TCM 1129, Dec. 24,978(M), TC Memo, 1961-228; *C. F. Dinkins* 45 TC 593 (1966), aff'd 378 F.2d 825, 67-1 USTC 9452 (CA-8, 1967).

6

Repair Allowance

6.1 The Capital-Expense Gray Area

The Class Life ADR System attempts to solve one of the long-standing problems confronting taxpayers, the differentiation between the deduction of current period expenses and the capitalization of asset acquisitions, through a device called the "repair allowance."* Understanding the repair allowance requires some background in this capital-expense conflict.

The Internal Revenue Code requires different treatment for expenses than for capital expenditures,[1] though the Code itself does not adequately define either term. In general, however, expenditures that substantially prolong the life of an asset or are made to increase its value or adapt it to a different use are capital expenditures, while expenditures that do not substantially prolong the life of an asset or materially increase its value or adapt it for a substantially different use are expenses deductible in the year paid or incurred.[2]

Expenditures may have characteristics both of deductible expenses and capital expenditures. Thus, there is a considerable gray area, which is often a source of controversy between taxpayers and the Internal Revenue Service.[3] These disputes invariably center on questions of fact and usually have to be negotiated on a time-consuming item-by-item approach. Total dollar amounts at stake are often substantial, so the Internal Revenue Service employs specially trained

*Feinschreiber, "How to Get Tax Benefits from the Repair Allowance,"*Prentice-Hall Tax Ideas,* Parag. 25,008.

engineer agents in addition to regular agents, while taxpayers call upon appraisers, architects, and engineers in addition to accountants and lawyers.

The Tax Reform Act of 1969 included a provision to alleviate the capital-expense controversy for one type of asset, railroad rolling stock except locomotives. Rehabilitation expenditures during a 12-month period can be deducted in an amount up to 20 percent of the basis of the rolling stock.[4] This provision is the progenitor of the repair allowance, but substantial modifications have taken place.

The repair allowance was originally adopted by regulation as part of the Asset Depreciation Range (ADR) System promulgated early in 1971.[5] The Revenue Act of 1971 subsequently provided statutory backing for the repair allowance.*

6.2 Eligibility for the Repair Allowance

Use of the repair allowance is optional,[6] but it is available only to taxpayers who elect the Class Life ADR System.[7] Unlike other facets of the Class Life ADR System, the repair allowance is not limited to property acquired in 1971 or thereafter.[8] The following three exceptions limit the scope of the repair allowance:

1. If the special 20-percent railroad rolling stock repair allowance is used during a particular year, the regular repair allowance is not available for that class.[9]

2. The repair allowance does not apply to property that is repaired, rehabilitated, or improved for sale to customers.[10]

3. If a taxpayer follows the practice of acquiring property in need of rehabilitation, repair, or rebuilding to be suitable for its intended use, and makes expenditures to repair, rehabilitate, or improve the property so as to take advantage of the repair allowance, the repair allowance will not be available.[11]

To be eligible for the repair allowance, property must constitute repair allowance property.[12] The determination of repair allowance property is made separately for each guideline class.[13] Repair allowance property means property that is eligible for Class Life ADR depreciation or would have been eligible for Class Life ADR depreciation except that it had been placed in service before 1971.[14] The repair allowance applies to a guideline class only if a repair allowance percentage is in effect for that class for the taxable year.[15]

The Class Life ADR System provides limited exclusions for used

---

*For a discussion of the repair allowance within the context of the Class Life System, see Feinschreiber, "How and When to Use Class Life Depreciation," *Prentice-Hall Tax Ideas,* Parag. 15,020 at 15,020.8.

property,[16] property subject to amortization,[17] real property,[18] subsidiary assets,[19] property subject to the prerestoration period investment credit,[20] and property with a carryover basis.[21] These exclusions do not apply to the repair allowance so that these assets are treated as repair allowance property.

Where repair, maintenance, rehabilitation, or improvement expenditures during a taxable year exceed the repair allowance ceiling, so that the excess is treated as a property improvement (see *Section 6.3*), this property improvement is treated as repair allowance property for the purpose of computing the repair allowance ceiling in future taxable years.[22]

6.3 How the Repair Allowance Works

If the repair allowance is elected, amounts paid or incurred for repairs, maintenance, rehabilitation, or improvement of property are deductible up to an amount called the "repair allowance ceiling," which is the mathematical product of the dollar amount of repair allowance property times the repair allowance percentage. Any amount above this ceiling must be capitalized. These capitalized amounts are called "property improvements" and are placed in "special basis vintage accounts."

To generate the repair allowance ceiling, the repair allowance percentage is multiplied by the amount of repair allowance property in a guideline class. Repair allowance percentages are revised from time to time, and new percentages are also established. The original percentages were set forth in Rev. Proc. 72-10.

Table 12 gives a few examples of repair allowance percentages, listed in order from highest to lowest.

TABLE 12

Assets	Allowance, %	Assets	Allowance, %
Automobiles	16.5	Petroleum refining	7.0
Office equipment	15.0	Glass manufacture	6.0
Aircraft	14.0	Machinery manufacture	5.5
Construction equipment	12.5	Textile mill products	4.5
Farm machinery	11.0	Manufacture of vegetable oil products	3.5
Lumber-cutting equipment	10.0	Cement manufacture	3.0
Ferrous-metal manufacturing facilities	8.0	Office furniture	2.0
		Water utilities	1.5

There are no repair allowance percentages for many guideline classes, including buildings, various communication classes, and farm animals.

The repair allowance percentage in effect on the last day of the taxable year applies for that taxable year.[23] However, the repair allowance percentage initially effective for the taxable year can be used if higher.[24] Use of the repair allowance is elected annually.

The repair allowance is limited to the repair allowance ceiling, which is the amount of repair allowance property[25] multiplied by the repair allowance percentage in effect for the asset guideline class for the taxable year.[26] This computation is actually somewhat complex because of the treatment of retirements in computing repair allowance property.

The repair allowance property in the asset guideline class at the beginning of the taxable year is averaged with the repair allowance property in the class at the end of the taxable year.[27] All property is measured by its unadjusted basis, which is the original basis in the hands of the taxpayer without reduction for depreciation.[28] From both the beginning-of-year balance and the end-of-year balance, the unadjusted basis of all property in a vintage account previously retired in ordinary retirements is subtracted.[29] The reason for this adjustment is that the unadjusted basis is not removed from a vintage account in the case of an ordinary retirement, although the basis adjustment is made in the case of an extraordinary retirement.[30]

Table 13 illustrates one method of computing the repair allowance ceiling. Here the guideline class consists of office equipment.

A special rule applies to buildings that are Section 1250 property. Each building is treated as in a separate guideline class unless all buildings are operated as an integrated unit.[31] Whether two or more buildings are treated as an integrated unit is evidenced by their actual operation, management, financing, and accounting.[32]

TABLE 13

Property at beginning of year	$100,000
Property retired in previous years	20,000
Net amount at beginning of year	$ 80,000
Purchases during the year	30,000
Retirements during the year	−18,000
Net amount at end of year	$ 92,000
Average amount	86,000
Repair allowance percentage	15.0
Repair allowance ceiling	$ 12,900

6.4 Excluded Additions

Certain expenditures are considered to be so clearly capital in nature that they are not deductible, even if they come within the repair allowance ceiling.[33] These items are called "excluded additions" and must be capitalized in any event.[34] Identifying items that constitute excluded additions is a complex question of fact that is a major stumbling block to effective use of the repair allowance. Separating expenditures eligible for the repair allowance from those that constitute excluded additions requires application of seven tests, five safe-haven rules, many definitions, and nine examples with a total of 34 illustrations.

The crucial facet of the excluded additions category is the term "identifiable unit of property," or IUP for short.[35] Such a unit of property generally is a separate machine or piece of equipment that performs a discrete function, is customarily acquired by the taxpayer as a unit, and is customarily retired by the taxpayer as a unit.[36] A taxpayer's accounting classification of units of property will generally be accepted by the Internal Revenue Service if the classification is reasonably consistent with the foregoing definition of units of property and if the taxpayer's classification procedure is consistently applied.[37]

Seven fact patterns indicate excluded additions:

1. A substantial increase in the productivity of an existing IUP over its productivity when first acquired by the taxpayer.[38]

2. A substantial increase in the capacity of an existing IUP over its capacity when first acquired by the taxpayer.[39]

3. Modification of an existing IUP for a substantially different use.[40]

4. Acquisition of an IUP that is either (1) an additional IUP[41] or (2) replacement of an IUP through retirement.[42]

5. Replacement of a part, component, or portion of an IUP if gain or loss is recognized on the replacement or is deferred under the consolidated return provisions.[43]

6. In the case of a building or other structure, any addition of cubic or linear space.[44]

7. In the case of pipelines, utilities, telephone companies, and telegraph companies, replacement of a material portion of a line, cable, or pole.[45]

The enumeration of identifiable units of property may prove elusive and may make the preceding 7 tests difficult to apply. In some cases, a unit of property may also be a component, portion, or part of another unit of property. Under some tests it will be treated as an IUP, while under others it will be treated as a component. The application of the rules concerning IUP can be demonstrated by the following example pertaining to automobiles.

Where a taxpayer owns a fleet of 5 automobiles, each automobile is an IUP.[46] The fleet of cars is not an IUP.[47] When one automobile is retired and replaced, the replacement vehicle is an IUP and therefore an excluded addition.[48] Also, the purchase of a sixth automobile is an expenditure for an additional IUP and is an excluded addition.[49]

An addition of an airconditioner to an automobile is an excluded addition,[50] but the replacement of an existing airconditioner is not an excluded addition.[51] The reason for this distinction is that, in the case of acquisitions, an item that is an IUP but which is also a component of another IUP is treated as an IUP and not as a component.[52] In the case of replacements, it is treated as a component.[53] If an IUP (such as the automobile airconditioner in this illustration) is retired in a transaction where gain is recognized, or would be recognized but for a deferral provision in the consolidated return regulations, its character as an IUP predominates over its character as a component, so the replacement is an excluded addition.[54]

There are five safe-haven rules that can be useful in differentiating excluded additions from expenditures eligible for the repair allowance: (1) small expenditures, (2) small increases in capacity, (3) small increases in productivity, (4) mere extension of productive life, and (5) a special rule for transmission utilities.

The first safe-haven rule enables taxpayers to avoid treating certain small expenditures as excluded additions. An excluded addition does not include an expenditure in connection with the repair, maintenance, rehabilitation, or improvement of an IUP when the cost does not exceed $100.[55] All related expenditures with respect to the IUP must be grouped together for this purpose.[56] However, this safe-haven does not apply to the purchase of an additional IUP or the replacement of an IUP.[57]

The second and third safe-haven rules for excluded additions apply to increases in capacity or productivity.[58] For this purpose, an increase in productivity or capacity is substantial only if the increase is more than 25 percent.[59] This rule is a major advantage of the repair allowance as compared with a facts-and-circumstances determination. Note that this increase is based on the productivity or capacity of the IUP when first acquired by the taxpayer, not the productivity or capacity immediately before the expenditure.[60] Consider the following example:

Capacity when acquired	100 widgets per hour
Capacity before rebuilding	80 widgets per hour
Capacity after rebuilding	125 widgets per hour

The expenditure to rebuild the asset does not constitute an excluded addition because the capacity after rebuilding does not exceed 25 percent. Of course, substantiation of capacity or productivity figures will usually not be this easy. In fact, in some cases it will present an insurmountable obstacle. Substantiation of productivity or capacity is made more difficult to achieve because neither "productivity" nor "capacity" is defined in the repair allowance regulations. The inventory costing regulations refer to both theoretical capacity and practical capacity,* but it is uncertain what is meant in this context.

A further interpretive problem arises when some expenditures are made in one year and some in a later year so that the increase in capacity or productivity is less than 25 percent in any one year but more than 25 percent in aggregate. Does the second expenditure taint the first, causing both to fall outside the safe-haven test? The solution may depend on whether there was a concerted plan for the second expenditure at the time the first was undertaken.

Another safe-haven rule is an important factor in making the repair allowance advantageous: An expenditure that merely extends the productive life of an IUP is not treated as an excluded addition.[61]

A special safe-haven rule applies to pipelines, electric utilities, telephone companies, and telegraph companies.[62] For such organizations, a replacement of lines, cables, or poles is material only if the portion replaced exceeds 5 percent of the lines, cables, or poles that constitute a unit of property.[63] A unit of property in such a case generally consists of each segment that performs a discrete function, either as to capacity, service, transmission, or distribution between identifiable points.[64]

A special definitional rule applies to the determination of IUP in the case of a building. The IUP generally consists of the building as well as its structural components except that each building service system (such as an elevator, an escalator, the electrical system, or the heating and cooling system) is an IUP for purposes of the definition of excluded addition with respect to productivity, capacity, modification, acquisition of additional units, and normal retirements.[65]

If an expenditure does constitute an excluded addition and is eligible for Class Life ADR depreciation, the excluded addition is capitalized in a vintage account.[66]

The examples in Table 14 (on the next page) illustrate the application of the rules for determining excluded additions.

---

*Feinschreiber, "How Extensive Are the Absorption Costing Requirements in the Final Inventory Regs.?" *Journal of Taxation,* December 1973, pp. 338–341.

TABLE 14

Expenditure	Excluded Addition
Example 1: Machine Shop	
1. $5,000 for general maintenance (inspection, oiling, machine adjustments, cleaning, and painting)	No
2. $175 for replacement of bearings and gears in an existing lathe	No
3. $125 for replacement of an electric stacker and wiring in a drill press	No
4. $300 for modification of a metal fabricating machine which substantially increases its capacity	Yes
5. $175 for repair of the same machine which does not substantially increase its capacity	No
6. $800 for the replacement of an existing lathe with a new lathe	Yes
7. $65 for the repair of a drill press	No
Example 2: Steel Plant	
1. Reline open-hearth furnace	No
2. Place 20 new ingot molds in service	Yes
3. Replace one reversing roll in blooming mill	No
4. Overhaul rail and billet mill with no increase in capacity	No
5. Replace a roll stand in 20-inch bar mill	Yes
6. Overhaul increases billet speed from 1,800 feet per minute to 2,300 feet per minute	Yes
Example 3: Warehouse	
1. $1,000 for two new temporary partitions	Yes
2. $1,400 for repainting the exterior of a building	No
3. $300 for roof repair	No
4. $150 for replacement of two window frames and panes in a warehouse	No
5. $100 for plumbing repair	No
Example 4: Factory	
1. $10,000 for expansion of a loading dock from 600 square feet to 750 square feet	Yes
2. $600 for replacement of two roof girders in a factory building	No

TABLE 14 (continued)

Expenditure	Excluded Addition
3. $9,500 for replacement of columns and girders to increase by 50 percent the weight of supplies that can be stored	Yes

Example 5: Office Building

1. $400,000 to replace 5 manual elevators with high-speed automatic elevators	Yes
2. $1,700 to replace the cable in one of the existing elevators	No

Example 6: Cement Plant

1. Replace part of gyratory crusher	No
2. Place new apron feeder and hammer mill in service	Yes
3. Replace four buckets on chain bucket elevator	No
4. Reline kiln	No
5. Install additional dust collectors	Yes
6. Replace conveyor belts	No

Example 7: Pipeline Company

1. Replace a meter on a gas well	Yes
2. Replace a 3,000-foot section of a 2-mile pipeline	Yes
3. Replace a 2,000-foot section of a 100-mile pipeline	No
4. Replace a 7-mile section of a 100-mile pipeline	Yes

Example 8: Utility Company

1. Replace 25 of 300 utility poles	Yes
2. Replace transformer on one pole	Yes
3. Replace a crossarm on one pole	No
4. Replace 200-foot section of 2-mile circuit	No

Example 9: Telephone Company

1. Replace 100 feet of 8 miles of telephone cable	No
2. Replace amplifier in distribution system	Yes
3. Replace 10 miles of a 50-mile cable	Yes

The repair allowance will be most beneficial to taxpayers that make expenditures similar to those in Example 2, No. 4, and Example 6, No. 4 and 6, because these expenditures come within the "gray area" and are sometimes capitalized on audit by the Internal Revenue Service when repairs are based on facts and circumstances.

6.5 Property Improvements and Special Basis Vintage Accounts

If the repair allowance is elected and included expenditures exceed the repair allowance ceiling, the excess is termed a "property· improvement."[67] The total amount of property improvements in an asset guideline class is capitalized in a single "special basis vintage account" for that taxable year.[68] This amount is depreciated over the asset depreciation period for the account.[69]

The Class Life ADR Regulations provide rules for the treatment of property improvements in the event that the repair allowance is not elected or that certain assets do not constitute repair allowance property.[70] In that event, "property improvement" is defined as an expenditure that is treated as a capital expenditure.[71] Such a property improvement, if it is eligible for Class Life ADR depreciation, must be capitalized in the applicable vintage account.[72]

Expenditures in excess of the repair allowance ceiling must be capitalized as property improvements.[73] These amounts are capitalized in a special basis vintage account.[74] This amount is to be depreciated over the asset depreciation period for the account.

Normally, the unadjusted basis, adjusted basis, and depreciation reserve are not allocated to specific assets.[75] However, where repair allowance property is retired in an abnormal retirement or an extraordinary retirement, it is possible to, in essence, retire a portion of ·the special basis vintage account if this technique is consistently applied.[76] The allocation is to be based on the adjusted basis of the repair allowance property in the asset guideline class at the beginning of the year.[77]

6.6 Interrelationship with the Inventory Costing Regulations

The repair allowance would enable various expenditures to be treated as expenses rather than as capital items.[78] Certainly, this rule would apply to both repairs and maintenance. Indirect materials and supplies should also be encompassed within this provision.[79]

The inventory costing regulations require that these items be inventoried rather than expensed.[80] Thus, expenditures for repairs, maintenance, and indirect materials and supplies are deductible only when they become part of cost of goods sold.*

Thus, conflicts between the repair allowance and the inventory costing provisions can be expected. However, the two regulations

*Feinschreiber, "How Extensive Are the Absorption Costing Requirements in the Final Inventory Regs.?" *Journal of Taxation,* December 1973, pp. 338–341.

can be read together in the following manner: The repair allowance provisions determine whether or not an expenditure is capital in nature. If it is determined that an expenditure is noncapital, the inventory costing regulations determine whether the amount is inventoried or is treated as a period expense.

6.7 Recordkeeping Requirements

A taxpayer electing to use the repair allowance provisions is specifically required to maintain adequate books and records.[81] These books and records must generate two categories of information: First, the books and records must be reasonably sufficient to determine expenditures for repairs, maintenance, rehabilitation, or improvements of repair allowance property.[82] This information must be generated for each asset guideline class and for each taxable year. Secondly, books and records must be sufficient to isolate excluded additions.[83]

Recordkeeping requirements are inherently great where expenditures overlap different guideline classes or where expenditures are made for nonrepair allowance property as well as repair allowance property.[84] However, allocation of the expenditures may be allowed where books and records do not identify these expenditures with either specific items of property or groups of similar properties.[85] Allocation is allowed only where it is not practical to identify these expenditures with specific items of property or groups of similar properties.[86] In such a case, the total amount of expenditure that is not specifically so identified may be allocated by any reasonable method, provided the allocation method is consistently applied.[87]

Where the repair, maintenance, rehabilitation, or improvement is made by a company's production personnel, the costs may be allocated.[88] The allocation method must be reasonable and must also be consistently applied.[89] When a company's production personnel are used for these services, the prerequisite for allocation—that it not be practical to identify expenditures with specific items of property or groups of similar properties—need not be met.[90] Further, if services performed by the company's production personnel are both incidental to production and not substantial in amount, no allocation need be made to the repair, maintenance, rehabilitation, or improvement category.[91]

In the general situation where rehabilitation or improvements are not made by production personnel, the availability of allocation depends upon whether the expenditures are of the type that would be specifically identified with specific items of property or groups of similar properties.[92] The expenditures that would normally be *specifically identified* are:

1. Substantial expenditures such as for major parts or major structural materials for which a work order is or would customarily be written.

2. Expenditures for work performed by an outside contractor.

3. Expenditures under a specific downtime program.

Other expenditures that would be *allocated* rather than specifically identified are:

1. General maintenance costs of machinery, equipment, and plant in the case of a taxpayer having assets in more than one class (or different types of assets in the same class) which are located together or generally maintained by the same work crew.

2. Small supplies that are used with respect to various classes or types of property.

3. Labor costs of personnel who work on property in different classes, or different types of property in the same class, if the work is performed on a routine as-needed basis and the only identification of the property repaired is by the personnel.

Where expenditures are eligible for allocation and are allocated by the taxpayer, the allocation must be reasonable. The Internal Revenue Service uses a minimum of four factors in determining if the allocation is reasonable:[93] (1) the prior experience of the taxpayer, (2) the relative basis of the assets in the guideline class, (3) the types of assets involved, and (4) the relationship to specifically identified expenditures.

The taxpayer should be cautioned that these allocations, and even the meaning of the term "allocation," do not coincide with the international source-of-deductions rules of Section 1.861-8 of the Regulations* or the inventory costing regulations of Section 1.471-11 of the Regulations. However, these latter two regulations are not consistent with each other either.

6.8 Application of the Repair Allowance

The repair allowance was designed to eliminate controversy over the capital-expense categorization, but as our analysis concluded, this objective was achieved only in part. There are four principal reasons

---

*Bodner and Feinschreiber, "Introducing the Proposed Regulations for Allocating and Apportioning Deductions," *U.S. Taxation of International Operations,* August 10, 1973, ¶6002; Hammer and Crawford, "Proposed Source of Income Regulations: Increased Double Taxation," *Tax Adviser,* October 1973, pp. 590–597.

why the repair allowance fails to reach its stated goals and why few taxpayers have adopted it to date:

1. The repair allowance is inordinately complex.
2. The repair allowance has failed to clearly resolve controversies between capital and expense.
3. The repair allowance percentages are too low, so that a portion of the bona fide repair expenses would have to be capitalized as property improvements.
4. The recordkeeping requirements are too burdensome.

Hopefully, changes in the repair allowance regulations will be made so that they will become more easily applied to depreciation computations by American business and industry.

The primary advantage to the repair allowance that has enabled it to achieve some use is that it can be elected for some guideline classes and not others, and that it can be used in some taxable years but not others.

REFERENCES

1. IRC Sec. 162, Sec. 212, and Sec. 263.
2. 11(d)(2)(i)(a).
3. *Cincinnati, New Orleans and Texas Pacific Ry. Co.* (Ct. Cl. 1970), 424 F.2d 563, 25 AFTR2d 70–988.
4. IRC Sec. 263(e).
5. T. D. 7128, June 22, 1971.
6. 11(d)(2)(ii).
7. 11(a)(1).
8. 11(d)(2)(iii), 11(b)(2)(ii).
9. 11(d)(2)(v)(b).
10. 11(d)(2)(v)(c)(1).
11. 11(d)(2)(v)(c)(2).
12. 11(d)(2)(ii).
13. 11(d)(2)(ii).
14. 11(d)(2)(iii), 11(b)(2)(ii).
15. 11(d)(2)(iii).
16. 11(b)(5)(iii), 11(d)(2)(iii).
17. 11(b)(5)(v).
18. 11(b)(5)(vi).
19. 11(b)(5)(vii).
20. 11(b)(5)(iv).
21. 11(b)(7).
22. 11(d)(2)(vii)(a), 11(d)(2)(iii).
23. 11(d)(2)(iii).
24. 11(d)(2)(iii).
25. 11(d)(2)(iii)(a).
26. 11(d)(2)(iii)(b).
27. 11(d)(2)(iii)(a).
28. 11(d)(2)(iii)(a).
29. 11(d)(2)(iii)(a).
30. 11(d)(3)(iii), 11(d)(3)(iv).
31. 11(d)(2)(iii).
32. 11(d)(2)(iii).
33. 11(d)(2)(i)(a).
34. 11(d)(2)(viii).
35. 11(d)(2)(vi).
36. 11(d)(2)(vi).
37. 11(d)(2)(vi).
38. 11(d)(2)(vi)(a).
39. 11(d)(2)(vi)(b).
40. 11(d)(2)(vi)(c).
41. 11(d)(2)(vi)(d)(1).
42. 11(d)(2)(vi)(d)(2).
43. 11(d)(2)(vi)(e).
44. 11(d)(2)(vi)(f).
45. 11(d)(2)(vi)(g).
46. 11(d)(2)(vi).
47. 11(d)(2)(vi).
48. 11(d)(2)(vi)(d)(2).
49. 11(d)(2)(vi)(d)(1).
50. 11(d)(2)(vi)(d)(1).
51. 11(d)(2)(vi)(d)(2).
52. 11(d)(2)(vi).
53. 11(d)(2)(vi).
54. 11(d)(2)(vi)(e).
55. 11(d)(2)(vi).
56. 11(d)(2)(vi).

57. 11(d)(2)(vii)(*d*), (*e*).
58. 11(d)(2)(vi)(*a*), (*b*).
59. 11(d)(2)(vi).
60. 11(d)(2)(vi).
61. 11(d)(2)(vi).
62. 11(d)(2)(vi)(*g*).
63. 11(d)(2)(vi).
64. 11(d)(2)(vi).
65. 11(d)(2)(vi).
66. 11(d)(2)(viii)(*c*).
67. 11(d)(2)(iv)(*a*), 11(d)(2)(vii)(*a*).
68. 11(d)(2)(viii)(*a*).
69. 11(d)(3)(vi).
70. 11(d)(2)(iv)(*b*).
71. 11(d)(2)(vii)(*b*).
72. 11(d)(2)(viii)(*b*).
73. 11(d)(2)(viii)(*a*).
74. 11(d)(3)(vi).
75. 11(d)(3)(vi).

76. 11(d)(3)(vi).
77. 11(d)(3)(vi).
78. 11(d)(2)(v)(*a*).
79. 11(d)(2)(v)(*a*).
80. Reg. Sec. 1.471-11(c)(1).
81. 11(d)(2)(v)(*a*).
82. 11(d)(2)(v)(*a*)(*1*).
83. 11(d)(2)(v)(*a*)(*2*).
84. 11(d)(2)(v)(*a*).
85. 11(d)(2)(v)(*a*).
86. 11(d)(2)(v)(*a*).
87. 11(d)(2)(v)(*a*).
88. 11(d)(2)(v)(*a*).
89. 11(d)(2)(v)(*a*).
90. 11(d)(2)(v)(*a*).
91. 11(d)(2)(v)(*a*).
92. 11(d)(2)(v)(*a*).
93. 11(d)(2)(v)(*a*).
94. 11(d)(2)(ii).

7

Asset Retirements

7.1 Introduction

The tax accounting treatment of asset retirements is a complex subcategory of tax depreciation. The initial source of complexity is the existence of three different sets of asset retirement rules. Thus, there are separate technical rules for each of the three depreciation systems now in effect:

1. The Class Life ADR System, if elected, for assets placed in service in 1971 or thereafter (see *Section 7.2*).
2. The Guideline Class Life System, if elected, for assets placed in service in 1970 or prior years (see *Section 7.4*).
3. Facts-and-circumstances depreciation, if the Class Life ADR System or the Guideline Class Life System has not been elected (see *Section 7.3*).

The tax accounting rules that govern an asset retirement are determined in advance, generally upon asset acquisition, not on retirement. The applicable tax accounting treatment is, in essence, elected when the decision to adopt or reject Class Life ADR depreciation is made.*

*Feinschreiber, "How to Account for Asset Retirements Under the ADR Class Life System," *Prentice-Hall Tax Ideas*, ¶25,033.

This chapter first examines the asset retirement rules applicable to the Class Life ADR System and then considers the retirement rules utilized within the other two depreciation systems. Finally, various tax-planning strategies are considered.

7.2 Retirements Within the Class Life ADR System

Retirement of assets subject to the Class Life ADR System has not yet been of major importance because the system began in 1971 and there have been relatively few retirements of assets under its purview. As the Class Life ADR System and assets within it mature and assets are retired, these provisions will become increasingly important.

An intricate set of asset retirement rules has been developed for the Class Life ADR System. The general structure of these rules is to establish criteria for determining when a retirement takes place, to delineate a distinction between ordinary and extraordinary retirements, and then to provide differing tax treatment for these two different types of asset retirements. Additional facets of the Class Life ADR retirement rules include special rules for certain types of retirements, such as those involving mass assets, consolidated returns, or transfers between related parties. There are also rules applicable to capitalized repairs and to various reductions in salvage value because of retirements.

It should be noted at the outset that the cost of removing, dismantling, or demolishing an asset as part of a retirement from a vintage account is a deductible expense in the year paid or incurred.[1] Consequently, this cost is not subtracted from the reserve as a reduction of actual salvage value proceeds.[2] The Regulations use the term "incurred," but context would indicate that "accrued" is meant.

7.2.1 Determining When an Asset Is Retired

In many cases, asset retirement is an obvious fact, or at least readily ascertainable. In other cases, retirement appears to be a gradual process. Older assets may decline in usefulness and in use until productivity ceases altogether. Or, an asset may be put in a back room and held in reserve in case of emergency. Neither the gradual retirement nor the asset placed in reserve constitutes an asset retirement for purposes of the Class Life ADR System.

The Regulations provide that an asset is retired when permanently withdrawn from use.[3] The "use" to which the Regulations refer is use in a trade or business or in the production of income of the taxpayer.[4] In the two examples in the preceding paragraph, there was no permanent withdrawal from use, so there is no retirement under the Class Life ADR System.

Assets not currently used, such as idle plants, are not treated as retired and are subject to depreciation.[5] On the other hand, an abandonment is a retirement, so no further depreciation can be taken.[6]

The Regulations also delineate various events that constitute a retirement:[7]

1. Sale or exchange.
2. Other act of the taxpayer amounting to a permanent disposition of an asset.
3. Physical abandonment.
4. Transfer of an asset to supplies or scrap.

The second category is open-ended, so various different events can qualify as a retirement. In this regard, it would seem that involuntary permanent dispositions should qualify, but this may not be the result because the second category uses the term "act of the taxpayer." It is also relevant to note that the Regulations do not define either "permanent" or "disposition," other than to delineate the events listed above.

The definition of a retirement under facts-and-circumstances depreciation and Guideline Class Life depreciation are the same (see *Section 7.3.1* and *Section 7.4*).

7.2.2 Distinguishing Ordinary and Extraordinary Retirements

Asset retirements are classified as "ordinary" unless a specific rule causes the retirement to be categorized as "extraordinary."[8] There are three such specific rules concerning real property,[9] casualties,[10] and business curtailment.[11] Each of these three rules are discussed in turn in subsequent paragraphs.

Retirements of real property are extraordinary retirements. In more technical terms, the Regulations provide that the retirement of an asset that constitutes "Section 1250 property" is an extraordinary retirement.[12] "Section 1250 property" is a narrower concept than the term "real property." Excluded are land; special-purpose structures, research facilities, and storage facilities that qualify for the investment credit; elevators and escalators; and pollution control facilities, railroad grading and tunnel bores, on-the-job training facilities, and child-care facilities subject to 5-year amortization.[13]

The categorization of Section 1250 retirements as extraordinary and Section 1245 retirements (generally) as ordinary is disadvantageous to taxpayers in most circumstances. As we shall see in *Sections 7.2.3* and *7.2.4*, ordinary retirements generally do not give rise to recognition of gain or loss, while gain or loss is recognized in the case of extraordinary retirements. As a practical matter, retirements of real property are far more likely than retirements of personal property to give rise to gains, and far less likely to give rise to losses. Consequently, taxpayers will be realizing gains on extraordinary retirements of real estate which are subject to taxation on a current basis. On the other hand, these taxpayers will also be realizing losses on ordinary retirement of personal property items, but no current deductions will be allowed for these losses because of the nonrecognition rule applicable to ordinary losses. This whipsaw effect—gains are taxed while losses are not deductible—can in some circumstances be a significant drawback of the Class Life ADR System. Note that the mandatory recognition rule for Section 1250 property does not apply outside the Class Life ADR System.[14]

The Regulations provide that each taxpayer can elect to treat casualty retirements of personal property as extraordinary retirements.[15] The technical terminology used in the regulations to describe personal property is "Section 1245 property," which includes the various real property items enumerated above, except land, which are excluded from the Section 1250 category.[16] Casualty retirements include Section 1245 property retired as the direct result of fire, storm, shipwreck, or other casualty.[17] The definition here is identical with the definition of casualty for purposes of allowing the deduction for losses to individuals under Section 165(c)(3), except that theft losses are not included here. Note that the Regulations require the retirement to be a "direct result" of the casualty. The taxpayer has the burden of proof as to causality. Consequently, a taxpayer seeking extraordinary retirement treatment should maintain records to demonstrate that the retirement followed immediately from the casualty and would not have taken place but for the casualty.

A taxpayer seeking to avoid extraordinary retirement treatment also has the burden of proof. The term "direct result" may possibly have the same meaning as the legal term "proximate cause," but there is no specific authority for such conclusion. Also, if a taxpayer desires to treat certain casualty retirements as extraordinary, the taxpayer must treat other comparable casualty retirements in the same manner. This consistency requirement takes into account the type, the frequency, and the size of such casualties.[18]

In other words, a taxpayer may elect to treat major casualties as extraordinary and other casualties as ordinary. Presumably, the consistency requirement applies to retirements in various taxable years, not just to retirements within the same taxable year.

The final category of extraordinary retirement is the retirement of Section 1245 property (defined in preceding paragraphs) as the direct result of a business curtailment.[19] This retirement category includes four events: cessation, termination, curtailment, and disposition.[20] Not all forms of retirement (see *Section 7.2.1*) can be treated as extraordinary retirement; transfers to supplies or scrap are specifically excluded.[21] The curtailment rule applies to various forms or aspects of the enterprise: "business, manufacturing, or other income producing process, operation, facility or unit."[22]

There are two areas of complexity in applying the business cessation rule. First, the business curtailment rule utilizes the "direct result" test, which is also applicable to casualty retirements. Consequently, the taxpayer has the burden of proving or disproving that the retirement was extraordinary. In this regard, many taxpayers utilizing the Class Life ADR System have erroneously ignored the business cessation rule. Unlike casualty retirements, extraordinary retirement treatment on business cessation is not optional.

The second area of complexity in applying the business cessation rule to determine if a retirement is ordinary or extraordinary is a quantitative test. For such retirements to qualify as extraordinary,[23] more than 20 percent of the assets in an account must be retired during the taxable year as a direct result of business cessation. Assets are measured by their unadjusted basis (generally cost) without any reduction for depreciation except the additional first-year depreciation taken under Section 179.[24] Capitalized repairs that form a special basis vintage account (to be discussed in *Section 7.2.6*) are not taken into account for purposes of this computation.[25] In more technical terms, the test is expressed as a requirement that the unadjusted basis of all assets retired during the taxable year as the direct result of a business cessation event exceeds 20 percent of the unadjusted basis of such account immediately prior to such event.[26]

For purposes of the 20 percent test, similar asset accounts must be grouped together. More specifically, all assets acquired in the same taxable year and used in the same industry must be grouped together. In more technical terms, all accounts of the same vintage in the same asset guideline class must be treated as a single vintage account.[27]

The regulations provide two illustrations of the 20 percent rule for determining whether retirements resulting from a business cessation are extraordinary. In the first example, the taxpayer is a processor and distributor of dairy products owning six machines (Table 15)

TABLE 15

Machine	Unadjusted Basis	Function
X	$ 1,000	Bottle washing
Y	1,000	Bottle washing
Z	1,000	Bottle washing
E	10,000	Butter processing
S	10,000	Butter processing
C	1,000	Bottle capping
Total	$24,000	

acquired during the same taxable year.[28] Four machines, X, Y, Z, and C, are retired in a later year when the taxpayer changes from bottles to milk cartons. Sale of these machines is the direct result of the termination of a manufacturing process. However, the 20 percent test is not met ($4,000 divided by $24,000 is less than 20 percent), so the retirements are ordinary rather than extraordinary. This result would not be affected by X, Y, and Z being in item vintage accounts and machines E, S, and C being grouped together in a multiple-asset vintage account.

In the second example, a taxpayer retires milk delivery trucks as a result of eliminating home deliveries in the suburbs.[29] All trucks have the same unadjusted basis. Each vintage account is treated separately, since each was initiated in a different taxable year. Nevertheless, the 20 percent test is met in both cases and all retirements are extraordinary.

Vintage Account	Trucks in Account before Retirements	Retirements
1972	6	4
1974	6	2

In the preceding example, if only one truck had been retired from the 1974 vintage account, the 20 percent test would not be met and the retirement of that truck would not be extraordinary. The categorization of such retirement as ordinary would not affect the categorization of the retirements from the 1972 vintage account as extraordinary. Note that the vintage accounts are not combined, even though the assets are in the same guideline class, because the assets were acquired in different years.

There is an additional facet of the ordinary-extraordinary distinction: Certain ordinary retirements are recategorized as extraordinary if the retirement takes place in a nonrecognition transaction, if transferred to a related party during the year of acquisition, or if included in a consolidated return (see *Section 7.2.5*).

7.2.3 Treatment of Ordinary Retirements

The general approach of the Class Life ADR Regulations to ordinary retirements is virtually to pretend that they have not occurred and to continue to treat the account as if no event has taken place. Consequently, the asset remains in the account. In other words, the unadjusted basis of an asset retired in an ordinary retirement is not removed from the account, and the depreciation reserve for the account is not reduced by the depreciation allowable for the retired asset.[30] The previously unrecovered basis of the retired asset will be recovered through the allowance for depreciation with respect to the vintage account.[31] Proceeds from an ordinary retirement are added to the depreciation reserve of the vintage account in which the retired asset is recorded.[32] Thus, actual salvage value proceeds will ultimately affect the amount of depreciation allowable.

The "ordinary retirement" provision of the regulations generally provides for nonrecognition of gain or loss on asset disposition.[33] Loss is not recognized unless no assets remain in the vintage account after the retirement[34] (see *Section 7.2.8*). Gain is not recognized unless the retirement proceeds cause the depreciation reserve to exceed the unadjusted bases of the vintage account[35] (see *Section 7.2.8*).

Table 16 illustrates the effect of an ordinary retirement from a multiple asset vintage account. Here asset A was sold for $8,000. This illustration should be compared with the example in *Section 7.2.4*, where the retirement is treated as extraordinary. Note that gain is realized to the extent of $3,000—proceeds of $8,000 less adjusted basis of $5,000 (unadjusted basis of $10,000 less depreciation reserve of $5,000)—but this gain is not recognized until the account is closed. Instead, the proceeds are added to the reserve and may affect allowable depreciation. Consequently, in the case of an ordinary retirement,

TABLE 16

	Unadjusted Basis	Reserve
Entire account before retirement of asset A	$40,000	$20,000
Asset A is retired	10,000	5,000
Balance after retirement of asset A but before reflecting proceeds	40,000	20,000
Proceeds	—	8,000
Balance of account after retirement	$40,000	$28,000

it is not necessary to ascertain the depreciation reserve applicable to a specific asset.

There is also a mandatory salvage value reduction upon an ordinary retirement. This salvage value reduction[36] should be distinguished from the optional salvage reduction opportunities (see *Section 7.2.7*). The salvage value adjustment is inordinately complex. The following rules can be viewed as an instruction to taxpayers:[37]

1. Compute tax depreciation for the account for the taxable year without this salvage value adjustment.
2. Then determine the depreciation reserve for the account, including the depreciation for the taxable year computed in step 1.
3. From the unadjusted basis of the account, subtract the salvage value for the account before this reduction.
4. Subtract the unadjusted basis less salvage value (step 3) from depreciation reserve (step 2). The difference is the salvage value reduction.

Thus, to the extent the reserve exceeds the unadjusted basis less salvage value, salvage value is to be reduced, but not below zero. This reduction is then to be applied retroactively to the same taxable year. Thus, in the case of a vintage account with an unadjusted basis of $1,000 and salvage value of $100, salvage value is reduced to the extent that proceeds from ordinary retirements increase the depreciation reserve above $900. If proceeds increase the reserve to $1,000, salvage value is reduced to zero.[38]

This salvage value reduction applies only when substantial proceeds are added to the reserve and a major portion of the assets' lives have elapsed, so that a substantial amount of accumulated depreciation has been placed in the reserve account. Therefore, this salvage value reduction will not be of substantial importance until an additional few years have elapsed, during which time more depreciation and proceeds will be added to vintage account reserves. This salvage value adjustment is also applicable to extraordinary retirements.

Note that the ordinary retirement rules do not apply when the retirement is part of a nonrecognition transaction, when the transfer is to a related party during the year of acquisition, or when certain nonrecognition provisions apply[39] (see *Section 7.2.5*). Such retirements are reclassified as extraordinary.

7.2.4 Treatment of Extraordinary Retirements

The general approach of the Class Life ADR System to extraordinary retirements is to terminate depreciation and cause gain or loss to be recognized.[40] These rules, however, do not supersede the nonrecognition provisions of the Internal Revenue Code[41] (see *Section 7.2.5*). Unless a specific nonrecognition provision applies, gain or loss is subject to the depreciation recapture provisions of Section 1245 for personal property and Section 1250 for real property, and then to Section 1231, which provides capital gain or ordinary loss treatment for the net gain or loss.[42] Section 165, pertaining to the deduction of losses, may also be applicable.[43]

The depreciation averaging conventions, half-year and modified half-year, are also applicable to extraordinary retirements[44] (see *Section 7.2.9*).

If the asset retired in an extraordinary retirement is the only asset in a vintage account, or is the last asset in a vintage account, the retirement causes the account to terminate.[45] Thus, the general rules for computing gain or loss will apply to the difference between the amount realized and the adjusted basis (unadjusted basis less the depreciation reserve) of the asset. For example, if the unadjusted basis is $100,000 and accumulated depreciation is $80,000, the adjusted basis would be $20,000 ($100,000 less $80,000). If the proceeds are $15,000, loss of $5,000 is recognized ($20,000 less $15,000).

When the retired asset is neither the only asset in the account nor the last asset in the account, the unadjusted basis of the retired asset is removed from the unadjusted basis of the vintage account.[46] The depreciation reserve is also adjusted to reflect the retirement. The depreciation reserve for the account is reduced by the depreciation allowable for the retired asset.[47] Here, some computational complexities may result. The depreciation allowable for the retired asset may not be a pro rata share of the depreciation reserve because the reserve may include proceeds from normal retirements. Consequently, it would be preferable to identify proceeds and depreciation separately in computing the reserve. Where the reserve does not separately identify proceeds and annual depreciation charges, it may be necessary to recompute depreciation as if that asset were the only asset in the account.

The following example, taken from the regulations, illustrates the treatment of an extraordinary retirement from a multiple-asset vintage account.[48] Here, asset A was sold for $8,000.

	Unadjusted Basis	Reserve
The entire account before retirement of asset A	$40,000	$20,000
Retirement of asset A	10,000	5,000
Account after retirement of asset A	$30,000	$15,000

The gain on disposition is computed as follows:

Proceeds		$8,000
Unadjusted basis	$10,000	
Less reserve	5,000	
Adjusted basis		3,000
Gain realized		$5,000

Because proceeds were less than the unadjusted basis, the Section 1245 depreciation recapture provision causes the entire gain to be treated as ordinary income.[49] This illustration should be compared with the example of an ordinary retirement in *Section 7.2.3*.

Another example illustrates extraordinary retirement treatment when Section 1250 property is retired.[50] Here, the asset is qualified residential real property eligible for double declining balance depreciation.[51] The building has a cost of $200,000 and a life of 40 years. Two years depreciation had been taken prior to sale of the building for $220,000. Depreciation for the first year was $10,000 ($2/40 \times $200,000) and the adjusted basis was reduced to $190,000 ($200,000 − $10,000). Depreciation for the second year was $9,500 ($2/40 \times $190,000) and the adjusted basis was reduced to $180,500 ($190,000 − $9,500). Since the building is sold for $220,000, the total gain was $39,500 ($220,000 − $180,500). The next step is to find out how much of the gain is Section 1250 gain (depreciation recapture taxed as ordinary income) and how much of the gain is potentially capital gain under Section 1231. The Section 1250 gain is the depreciation taken in excess of straight-line depreciation. Straight-line depreciation is $5,000 per year ($1/40 \times $200,000) for a total of $10,000. Since actual depreciation ($19,500) exceeds straight-line depreciation ($10,000), the balance ($9,500) is ordinary income. The remainder of the gain ($39,500 − $9,500 = $30,000) is subject to Section 1231.

These retirement rules also apply to ordinary retirements reclassified as extraordinary because they occurred as part of a nonrecognition transaction in a transaction with a related party during the year of acquisition or in a transaction subject to certain consolidated return rules[52] (see *Section 7.2.5*).

The salvage value of adjustment described in *Section 7.2.3* for ordinary retirements is also applicable to extraordinary retirements.

7.2.5 Special Retirements

There are four types of special retirements: retirements in which gain or loss is not recognized in whole or in part, certain transfers between

companies in a consolidated return, transfers between related enti-
ties, and retirement of mass assets.[53] Each such special retirement is
discussed in subsequent paragraphs.

Turning first to nonrecognition provisions, we find that the Class
Life ADR System generally causes the nonrecognition provisions of
the Internal Revenue Code to apply in an unusual manner. Where
such a provision is applicable, a retirement that would otherwise
constitute an ordinary retirement is converted into an extraordinary
retirement.[54] Then, the nonrecognition provisions apply and determine what part, if any, of the realized gain or loss will be unrecognized (untaxed).

There is no general, all-inclusive enumeration of applicable nonrecognition provisions. However, the Regulations mention three specific nonrecognition provisions:

1. The swap of like kind property tax-free under Section 1031 of
   the Regulations.
2. Distributions under Section 337 by a corporation to its shareholders in connection with liquidation of the corporation.
3. Contribution of property to a corporation by its controlling
   shareholders under Section 351.

Other nonrecognition transactions not specifically enumerated by the
Regulations include tax-free mergers, acquisitions, spinoffs, splitups,
and splitoffs in a corporate context, various partnership transactions,
and other nonrecognition transactions.

When an ordinary retirement occurs, but gain or loss is not recognized in whole or in part because of a special nonrecognition section
of the Internal Revenue Code, the retirement is to be treated as an
extraordinary retirement. Consequently, no part of the proceeds from
the retirement is added to the depreciation reserve of the vintage
account. The following two examples illustrate the effect of this
recategorization:

In the first example, asset A is a machine which is transferred in a
tax-free transaction solely for stock of another company. The value of
that stock is $1,400.[55]

	Unadjusted Basis	Reserve
Entire account before retirement of asset A	$3,000	$2,100
Asset A is retired	1,000	700
Account after retirement of asset A	$2,000	$1,400

The gain of disposition is computed as follows:

Proceeds (value of stock)		$1,400
Unadjusted basis	$1,000	
Less reserve	700	
Adjusted basis		300
Gain realized		$1,100

This gain of $1,100, while realized, is not recognized by virtue of Section 351. Note that the unadjusted basis of the account is reduced by $1,000 and the reserve is reduced by $700.

In the second example, the facts are the same as in the first except that the consideration for the machine consists of stock worth $1,200 plus $200 cash rather than stock worth $1,400.[56] The effects from a depreciation standpoint are the same even though $200 of the gain is now recognized and treated as ordinary income by virtue of the depreciation recapture provisions.

Ordinary retirements are also converted into extraordinary retirements when the consolidated return provisions cause a sale between component companies not to be recognized.[57] Such a transaction results in deferred gain or loss within the meaning of Section 1.1502-13(c) of the Regulations unless the affiliated group has elected under subparagraph (3) of these Regulations not to defer gain or loss. If the retirement is treated as extraordinary, no part of the proceeds from the retirement is added to the depreciation reserve of the vintage account. Thus, if a machine with an adjusted basis of $300 is sold for $1,400 to another member of its affiliated group which files a consolidated return, the $1,100 gain will be deferred unless the nondeferral election has been made under Section 1.1502-13(c)(3) of the Regulations.[58]

If an asset is transferred during the year it is first placed in service, and the recipient is a related entity, a retirement that would otherwise be treated as an ordinary retirement will be recategorized as an extraordinary retirement.[59] The technical rules that define related party are the same rules that apply to prevent multiple benefits from additional first-year depreciation.[60] Since the complexity of these rules would require extensive examination and since their impact in this area is so limited, further discussion of them is omitted from this book.

The Class Life ADR Regulations have specific provisions for mass assets.[61] Mass assets include returnable containers, portable air and electric tools, jigs, dies, railroad ties, overhead conductors, hardware, textile spindles, and minor items of office, plant, and store furniture and fixtures.[62] To qualify as mass assets, a mass or group of individual items need not be homogeneous but must meet four tests:[63]

1. Each item must be minor in value relative to the total value of the mass or group.
2. The items must be numerous in quantity.
3. The items must usually be accounted for only on a total dollar or quantity basis.
4. Separate identification of the items must be impracticable.

These four tests are the general requirements for mass asset categorization and are also applicable to the investment credit. For Class Life ADR depreciation purposes, two additional requirements apply: It must be impracticable for the taxpayer to maintain records that can be used to establish the vintage of such assets as retirements occur,[64] but the taxpayer must supply other pertinent information to the Internal Revenue Service.[65]

Mass asset treatment is, in essence, the use of a mortality dispersion table to determine when retirements occur.[66] Thus, the taxpayer is required to indicate the type of mortality dispersion table used to substantiate the retirement of the mass assets.[67]

The retirement dispersion table must be "appropriate."[68] Such a mortality dispersion table may be based upon an acceptable sampling of the taxpayer's actual experience or upon other acceptable statistical or engineering techniques.[69] A taxpayer also has the option of using a standard mortality dispersion table prescribed by the Internal Revenue Service, but the taxpayer would then have to use the table for subsequent taxable years unless the Internal Revenue Service gives permission to change to another dispersion table or to actual identification of retirements.[70] On the Class Life ADR depreciation form, Form 4832, the taxpayer must indicate whether a standard mortality dispersion table or a table based on the taxpayer's own experience is being utilized.[71] At the time this book was written, the Internal Revenue Service had issued no mass asset standard retirement dispersion tables in recent years, but the older dispersion table for investment credit purposes may possibly be usable by some taxpayers.[72]

The four categories of special retirements provide limited planning opportunities because they pertain to infrequent situations. Nevertheless, they merit advance planning and careful consideration because the dollar amounts involved may sometimes be substantial.

7.2.6 Special Basis Vintage Accounts

If a taxpayer elects the repair allowance[73] (see Chapter 6) and amounts paid or incurred during the taxable year for the repair, maintenance, rehabilitation, or improvement of repair allowance property (assets in the Guideline Class, even when acquired prior to 1971) exceed the repair allowance for the Guideline Class, the balance is termed a "property improvement."[74] The amount of a property improvement is placed in an account called a "special basis vintage account."[75] For most purposes, a special basis vintage account is treated in the same manner as other vintage accounts. However, special basis vintage accounts are excluded from the 20-percent test to determine if an asset retirement is ordinary or extraordinary.[76]

Generally, a special basis vintage account is depreciated in the same manner as other vintage accounts. The unadjusted basis (original basis, without reduction for the depreciation reserve) is recovered over the asset depreciation period for the account.[77]

These capitalized repairs do not represent specific assets. Because tracing to specific assets would not be feasible, the Regulations provide that the unadjusted basis, depreciation reserve, and adjusted basis are not allocated to specific assets in the guideline class.[78] Although the taxpayer can elect to make this allocation in the event of sales, exchanges, or other dispositions of repair allowance property in an extraordinary retirement,[79] it cannot do so in the case of ordinary retirements because the Regulations do not recognize gain or loss on disposition in that case (see *Section 7.2.3*).

The repair allowance applies to property acquired before 1971 as well as assets acquired subsequently. The Class Life ADR System does not apply to such earlier acquisitions. Consequently, "extraordinary retirement" treatment does not apply. However, the retirement may be treated as an abnormal retirement (see *Sections 7.3.4 and 7.4*). The allocation of a special basis vintage account to such items or accounts applies when an abnormal requirement takes place, assuming the taxpayer has so elected.[80],*

If the allocation in the case of abnormal or extraordinary retirements is elected, consistency is required and adequate records must be maintained.[81] Additionally, the election to allocate basis in this manner is to be made on the tax return.[82] There is no specific form or place on the return for making this election so that the taxpayer must choose marginal or other available space for entering its notation.

The adjusted basis of a special basis vintage account is allocated in

*Lyon, "Depreciation: Class Life System for Pre-1971 Property," 295 T.M. A-21.

the following manner:[83] The adjusted basis of the retired asset, as of the beginning of the taxable year, is divided by the adjusted basis of all repair allowance property in the asset guideline class at the beginning of the taxable year. This quotient is then multiplied by the adjusted basis of all special basis vintage accounts for the guideline class. The product thus obtained is treated as an additional extraordinary retirement and is, in effect, added to the adjusted basis of the retired asset. The unadjusted basis, depreciation reserve, and adjusted basis of the special basis vintage account are correspondingly adjusted, as the following example illustrates:

Adjusted basis of retired asset	$10,000
Adjusted basis of entire guideline class	$90,000
Ratio	1/9
Adjusted basis of special basis vintage account	$ 900
Allocation of adjusted basis of special basis vintage account to asset retirement (1/9 × $900)	$ 100

The adjusted basis of the retired machine is increased by this $100 from $10,000 to $10,100. Correspondingly, the adjusted basis of the special basis vintage account is reduced by $100 from $900 to $800.

The allocation of a portion of the adjusted basis of a special basis vintage account to the adjusted basis of the retired asset in an extraordinary or abnormal retirement is not a common event because its two component parts—adoption of the repair allowance and extraordinary retirement—are both relatively uncommon, particularly the adoption of the repair allowance. See Chapter 6 for an analysis of this phenomenon.

7.2.7 Retirements Permit Salvage Value Reduction

As retirements occur in a vintage account, the salvage value estimated for the account gradually becomes excessive. There are two causes of this condition. First, the unadjusted basis of the account is actually reduced, as in the case of extraordinary retirements,[84] or would have been reduced but for the rule which requires the unadjusted basis of retired assets to be retained in the case of ordinary retirements.[85] Consequently, salvage value becomes disproportionate relative to unadjusted basis. Second, proceeds are added to the account in the case of ordinary retirements.[86] Since salvage value represents estimated proceeds, reduction in depreciation because of both salvage value and actual proceeds is tantamount to double counting. Consequently, the Regulations permit salvage value to be reduced as retirements occur.[87]

There are four alternative methods for reducing salvage value by virtue of asset retirements:

1. A taxpayer may reduce the salvage value for a vintage account by the salvage value attributable to the retired asset.[88]

2. A taxpayer may reduce the salvage value of a vintage account in the case of extraordinary retirements, but not in the case of ordinary retirements.[89] If this option is used, the salvage value for the vintage account is reduced by the salvage value attributable to the retired asset.

3. In the case of an ordinary retirement by transfer of an asset to supplies or scrap, the taxpayer may reduce the salvage value for the account by the salvage value attributable to the retired asset. The retired asset, in the supplies or scrap account, will have a zero basis. Alternatively, basis can be established as the salvage value amount, but a corresponding amount must be added to the reserve of the vintage account from which the retirement took place.[90] (For greater detail concerning this technique, see Chapter 5.) When this method is used for retirements not resulting in a transfer to supplies or scrap, salvage value attributable to the retired asset reduces salvage value for the account.[91]

4. The taxpayer may value an asset as it is retired into a scrap or supplies account, provided the valuation method is reasonable, consistently applied, does not exceed the unadjusted basis of the asset, and is adequately identified in the taxpayer's books and records.[92] Potentially acceptable methods include average cost, conditioned cost, and fair market value.[93] This valuation then sets the basis of the asset in the supplies or scrap account, and a corresponding amount is added to the reserve of the vintage account from which the retirement took place.[94] This technique is discussed in greater detail in Chapter 5.

A taxpayer also has the option of making no salvage value adjustments as retirements occur.[95] Even if that alternative is elected, the salvage value reductions described in *Section 7.2.3* must take place when ordinary retirements cause the reserve to exceed unadjusted basis less salvage value.

When salvage value is reduced as asset retirements occur, the portion of the salvage value for a vintage account attributable to a retired asset may be determined by multiplying the salvage value for the account by the ratio of the unadjusted basis of the retired asset to the unadjusted bases of the account.[96] Alternatively, salvage value of the retired asset can be determined by any other method that is consistently applied and reasonably reflects the portion of the salvage value for the account originally attributable to the retired asset.[97] In other words, salvage value may be determined individually for each asset.

7.2.8 Recognition of Gain or Loss

In general, retirement of an asset in an ordinary retirement does not give rise to recognition of gain or loss[98] (see *Section 7.2.3*). However, a rule within the Class Life ADR System provides that gain or loss is to be recognized in certain circumstances.[99] This rule also prescribes the characterization of the gain as ordinary or capital.[100]

This gain-or-loss recognition rule applies only to Section 1245 property (personal property). This rule does not state on its face that it applies only to ordinary retirements, not to extraordinary retirements, but two factors lead to the conclusion that it is so restricted. First, gain or loss is always recognized in an extraordinary retirement unless a statutory nonrecognition provision applies[101] (see *Section 7.2.4*), so this provision would be superfluous to the extraordinary retirement fact pattern. Second, retirements of Section 1250 property (real property) always give rise to extraordinary retirement treatment, although retirements of Section 1245 property can sometimes give rise to extraordinary retirement treatment[102] (see *Section 7.2.2*).

The gain recognition aspects of this rule work in the following manner: Depreciation for the taxable year and salvage value adjustments are taken into account first. Then, if at the end of the taxable year the reserve exceeds the unadjusted basis for the account, the entire amount of the excess is recognized as gain in that taxable year.[103] If this rule were not in the Regulations, the account would wind up with a negative adjusted basis. The depreciation reserve is then reduced by the same amount so that, after the reduction in the reserve, the reserve is equal to the unadjusted basis of the account and the adjusted basis of the account is equal to zero.[104] In later years, no further depreciation is allowable unless the reserve is reduced through a salvage value reduction (see *Section 7.2.7*).

If gain is recognized by virtue of this rule, it will initially constitute Section 1245 gain (depreciation recapture treated as ordinary income).[105] For purposes of this computation, the reserve is separated into its two basic components: accumulated depreciation and proceeds from retirements. To the extent the gain, together with prior Section 1245 gain, does not exceed accumulated depreciation, the entire gain is Section 1245 gain. If this gain, plus prior Section 1245

TABLE 17

Unadjusted basis		$1,000
Accumulated depreciation	$ 600	
Proceeds in the account	100	
Total reserve		700
Adjusted basis		300
Proceeds during the year		500
Gain		$ 200
Additional reserve	300	
New reserve	$1,000	

gain, exceeds accumulated depreciation, the excess will be Section 1231 gain unless other provisions apply.[106]

Table 17 illustrates the gain rule. The data constitutes the fact pattern at the end of the taxable year, excluding proceeds realized during the taxable year.[107]

If the proceeds were $1,100, the gain would be $800. This gain would be taxed as follows:

Gain	$800
Accumulated depreciation (recapture taxed as ordinary income)	600
Section 1231 gain	$200

There is also a loss recognition rule when the last asset in an account is retired. If the unadjusted basis exceeds the depreciation reserve when the list asset is retired, the balance is treated as a loss or as an additional depreciation deduction.[108] If the retirement occurs through a sale or exchange, the loss may be subject to Section 1231.[109] These Regulations do not delineate the differences between those potential tax results.

The loss recognition rule is generally applicable when assets are retired from the account prior to completion of the asset depreciation period. When the last asset is retired from the vintage account, the vintage account will be terminated.[110] To prevent the loss recognition rule from being used to circumvent the ordinary retirement rule pertaining to the deferral of losses (see *Section 7.2.3*), another rule requires the combining of vintage accounts for purposes of the loss recognition rule.[111]

All accounts—other than a special basis vintage account for amounts capitalized under the repair allowance (see *Section 7.2.6*)— of the same vintage in the same asset guideline class (assets similar in use acquired during the same year) are combined into a single multiple-asset vintage account, provided the asset depreciation period is

FIGURE 2

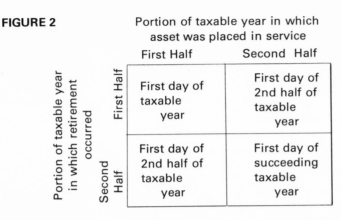

Portion of taxable year in which
asset was placed in service

	First Half	Second Half
First Half	First day of taxable year	First day of 2nd half of taxable year
Second Half	First day of 2nd half of taxable year	First day of succeeding taxable year

Portion of taxable year in which retirement occurred

the same for the accounts and the same depreciation method is used.[112] This rule does not indicate whether the depreciation method must be the same throughout the asset depreciation period, only at the end of the period, or when the accounts are considered for aggregation.

Both the gain rule and the loss rule will find increasing applicability as asset accounts subject to the Class Life ADR System mature and are retired.

7.2.9 Averaging Conventions Applicable to Retirements

Averaging conventions are applicable to asset retirements where losses on retirements are taken into account, that is, extraordinary retirements or, in limited situations, ordinary retirements. Averaging conventions treat asset acquisitions and retirements, which actually occur throughout the taxable year, as occurring on one or more specific dates (see Chapter 4). The Class Life ADR System permits the use of two averaging conventions, one of which must be selected for acquisitions during a taxable year: the half-year convention and the modified half-year convention. If the half-year convention has been utilized for asset acquisitions, extraordinary retirements are treated as having occurred on the first day of the second half of the taxable year. Figure 2 illustrates the application of the modified half-year convention to retirements.[113]

7.3 Asset Retirements Under Facts-and-Circumstances Depreciation

When assets are not depreciated under the Class Life ADR System, retirements are subject to a complex set of rules. These rules provide numerous options and permit a wide variety of tax accounting alternatives. Consequently, these retirement rules should not be viewed as a unified system. In fact, the tax consequences of a retirement depend upon the form of the transaction, the reason for the retirement, the timing of the retirement, the type of useful life estimate employed for. depreciation purposes, and the type of account utilized for the asset.[114]

7.3.1 Determining When an Asset Is Retired

A retirement of an asset is the permanent withdrawal of the asset from use in the trade or business or production of income. Retirement may result from disposition (by sale,[115] exchange,[116] abandonment,[117]) or without disposition (such as placement in a supplies or scrap account).

The definition of "retirement" under facts-and-circumstances depreciation is identical with the definition of retirement under the Class Life ADR System (see *Section 7.2.1*) and with the definition of retirement under the Guideline Class Life System (see *Section 7.4*).[118] Consequently, a gradual decline in usefulness of an asset or the removal of an asset from production (where the asset is held in reserve) is not considered a retirement (see *Section 7.2.1*). Moreover, these assets continue to be depreciable, at least if they are temporarily rather than permanently idle, since they are considered as being used in the business.

7.3.2 Types of Accounts

When depreciation is based on facts and circumstances, a broad latitude of asset grouping is permitted. Asset accounts are generally described as follows:[119]

1. Item accounts, each containing a single asset.
2. Group accounts, each containing assets similar in kind with useful lives that are approximately the same.
3. Classified accounts, each containing assets similar in use but without regard to useful life.
4. Composite accounts, each containing assets grouped without regard to use and without regard to useful life.

Group, classified, or composite accounts may be further subdivided on the bases of location, cost, character, use, and other criteria at the option of the taxpayer.[120] The Internal Revenue Service previously opposed the use of a composite account for building components if the building is used rather than new, but such uses of composite accounts are now permissible if various requirements are met.[121,*]

Multiple-asset accounts (group, classified, or composite) can be either closed-end or open-end.[122] Open-end accounts are, in essence, permanent accounts. Assets are added to an open-end account during a number of years and retirements take place over a number of years, so there is always an account balance. Closed-end accounts, on the other hand, are accounts established in the year of acquisition. Since acquisitions in a later year will be placed in a separate account, retirements will eventually cause such an account to be "used up" and terminated.

The type of assets included within an account (item, group, classified, or composite) and treatment of an account as open-end or as closed-end may have an effect on the manner in which retirements are treated.

7.3.3 Effects of Asset Life on Treatment of Retirements

The Regulations permit two different applications of useful life data. The depreciation period may be the average useful life of the assets in the account.[123] This application is invariably chosen because it results in more rapid depreciation. Alternatively, the depreciation period may be the maximum expected life of the longest-lived asset contained in the account.[124] Retirements are treated in a different manner (see *Section 7.3.5*) if this alternative is applied.

When the maximum life alternative is utilized, a rule for determining maximum life must be taken into account. The Regulations state that experience with assets that have attained an exceptional or unusual age is to be disregarded in determining the maximum expected useful life of the longest-lived asset in a multiple-asset account.[125] The Regulations provide an example in which an occasional asset may last for 60 years, there are 50 assets, the expected period of usefulness ranges from 20 to 40 years, and the average life is 30 years. In the example, the asset(s) that last for 60 years may be disregarded.[126] The example is deficient in that it does not indicate the level at which an asset's survival becomes "occasional" or "exceptional and unusual." Thus, the taxpayer who may have prepared an asset retirement dispersion table or graph is left without guidance as to whether the upper 5, 10, or 1 percent may be disregarded. Conceivably, the 60-year figure was picked because it is twice the average life, but there is no other basis in the Regulations for concluding that maximum life can be assumed to be twice the average life.

*Feinschreiber, "Component and Composite Depreciation," 1 *Journal of Real Estate Taxation* 250 (Spring 1974).

7.3.4 Normal and Abnormal Retirements

Unlike the Class Life ADR System, where the distinction between ordinary and extraordinary retirements is determinative of the tax consequences, the distinction between normal and abnormal retirements under facts-and-circumstances depreciation is only one of many factors that affect the tax results emanating from an asset retirement.[127]

There are no fixed standards for determining whether a retirement is normal or abnormal. Instead, the decision is based on the appropriate facts and circumstances. The general rule is that a retirement is treated as normal unless the taxpayer can demonstrate that the withdrawal is abnormal.[128] Thus, the "abnormal retirement" categorization appears to be elective on the part of the taxpayer, in contrast with the "ordinary-extraordinary" distinction under the Class Life ADR System, which is a mandatory distinction required of both the taxpayer and the Internal Revenue Service, except for retirements caused by casualties (see *Section 7.2.2*).

To demonstrate that a retirement is abnormal rather than normal, the taxpayer must show that the withdrawal of the asset from service was caused by a factor not contemplated when setting the depreciation rate.[129] Consequently, taxpayers should determine in advance what various factors enter into their choices of useful life and depreciation rate. In other words, taxpayers should enumerate the specific "facts and circumstances" upon which they rely in making their depreciation decisions.

The Regulations illustrate how such a "contemplated factors" rule can be applied. A retirement is considered "normal" if made within the range of years taken into consideration in fixing the depreciation rate.[130] A retirement is considered "normal" if the asset has reached a condition at which, in the normal course of events, the taxpayer customarily retires assets from use in its business.[131] It is uncertain whether both tests must be met for a retirement to be treated as normal.

For a retirement to qualify as "abnormal," the asset must be withdrawn from use at a time earlier than that used to determine useful life, or the retirement must be due to circumstances not contemplated when setting the depreciation rate.[132] Situations that would result in abnormal retirements are retirements due to casualty and sudden loss of usefulness caused by extraordinary obsolescence.[133]

In general, the "abnormal retirement" category under facts-and-circumstances depreciation is larger than the "extraordinary retirement" classification under the Class Life ADR System. Nevertheless, some retirements classified as "normal" could be categorized as "extraordinary" rather than as "ordinary."

7.3.5 Accounting for Retirements, Gains, and Losses

There are actually three separate systems for accounting for gains and losses resulting from retirements. Two of these methods are relatively straightforward and are described in this section. The third method is quite complex and is described in *Section 7.3.6*. At the outset, however, it must be noted that either of the two methods described herein may be used only as long as, in the opinion of the Internal Revenue Service, it clearly reflects income.[134] Both methods are designed for multiple-asset accounts where retirements are numerous. The more complicated third method may be used as a matter of right.

The general rule in the case of multiple-asset accounts (whether group, classified, or composite) is to distinguish between normal and abnormal retirements.[135] In the case of a normal retirement, the full unadjusted basis is removed from the asset account and an equal amount is removed from the reserve.[136] Actual salvage value proceeds are added to the reserve.[137] A Revenue ruling has also approved this procedure.[138] The following example illustrates the application of this rule.

	Asset Balance	Reserve
Account before retirement	$10,000	$4,000
Retirement of asset A	−2,000	−2,000
Salvage value proceeds	—	300
Account after retirement	$ 8,000	$2,300

This rule does not adequately deal with the situation in which an asset is retired early, when the reserve is low. Suppose the preceding retirement had taken place when the reserve was only $1,000. A literal application of this retirement rule would yield the following result:

	Asset Balance	Reserve
Account before retirement	$10,000	$1,000
Retirement of asset A	−2,000	−2,000
Salvage value proceeds	—	300
Account after retirement	$ 8,000	−$ 700

A negative reserve may find no greater acceptance than does a negative basis. Consequently, gain may have to be recognized to the extent of $700 in the preceding example. Presumably, where the reserve is so low, this indicates that the retirement took place quite early during the life of the asset, so that abnormal retirement treatment may be appropriate. In the Class Life ADR System, this problem does not exist because the unadjusted basis is not deducted from the asset balance and the reserve. In fact, this specific problem may have caused the difference in tax accounting treatment.

There are two separate Regulations affecting this retirement.[139] One assumes, in essence, that all retirements are "normal."[140] The other Regulation recognizes the existence of "abnormal" retirements.[141] If a retirement is "abnormal," the unadjusted basis is removed from the asset account. There is a deduction from the reserve, but only for the amount of depreciation applicable to the asset.[142] Implicitly, gain or loss is recognized and is measured by the proceeds minus the unadjusted basis as reduced by applicable depreciation. Thus, in our example, if the reserve applicable to the asset is $800, loss would be determined as follows:

Proceeds		$ 300
Unadjusted basis	$2,000	
Reserve	800	
Adjusted basis		1,200
Gain (loss)		($ 900)

This particular tax accounting treatment is probably the most widespread method of accounting for gains and losses (outside the Class Life ADR System and the Guideline Class Life System) by a wide margin. However, another relatively simple method is also permissible, though it is rarely used.

In this second method, all proceeds are reflected as ordinary taxable income.[143] Thus, proceeds are taken into income immediately rather than gradually (or at the termination of the account) through lesser depreciation deductions. Consequently, this method has not found widespread favor with taxpayers. The applicable Regulation does not indicate whether the distinction between normal and abnormal retirements is recognized. In our example, the $300 proceeds would be reflected as gain, at least if the retirement is normal. Consequently, the adjusted basis of the account (asset balance less reserve) would remain unchanged, even if the unadjusted basis is removed from both. If abnormal retirements are not permitted under this rule, the transaction we would otherwise reflect as a $900 loss would have to be reflected as a $300 gain because the $1,200 adjusted basis would not be considered.

7.3.6 The Third Rule for Retirements, Gains, and Losses

When depreciation is based on facts and circumstances rather than on the Class Life ADR System or the Guideline Class Life System, retirements can be accounted for by a third method as an alternative to the two methods described in the preceding subsection. This retirement accounting procedure has five basic facets:

1. The transfer of assets to supplies or scrap, as distinguished from retirements by disposition.
2. The distinction between normal and abnormal retirements.
3. Adjustments to asset basis for computing gain or loss.
4. The use of maximum depreciation life compared with average depreciation life.
5. Mandatory grouping of asset accounts.

Unlike the two methods of accounting for asset retirements described in the preceding subsection, this method is not dependent on the discretion of the Internal Revenue Service and can be used as a matter of right by each taxpayer. Unfortunately, complexities of this method limit its practical applicability.

The first step in applying this retirement method is to distinguish between retirements by disposition of an asset and retirements resulting from the transfer of an asset into a supplies account. This analysis will initially examine retirements by disposition and then return to dispositions by transfer to supplies or scrap.

There are three enumerated types of retirement by disposition: arm's-length sale,[144] exchange,[145] and abandonment.[146] To constitute an abandonment, the taxpayer must intend to discard the asset so that it will never be used again by the taxpayer nor retrieved by the taxpayer for subsequent sale, exchange, or other disposition.[147] Additionally, the retirement must be actual and physical.[148] Condemnation of a building as unfit for further occupancy qualifies as an abandonment.[149]

A number of cases define "abandonment." A building demolished as a condition of a land sale did not give rise to an abandonment loss,[150] but in another case a barn was found to have been abandoned before the land on which it had been situated was sold.[151] There was no actual physical abandonment where a taxpayer intended to sell rather than demolish buildings.[152] Similarly, an abandonment loss was disallowed for office equipment that was subsequently sold by the taxpayer.[153] In another case, racetrack facilities were held to be abandoned.[154]

Generally, in the case of retirement by asset disposition, the recognition of gain or loss is subject to the regular recognition provisions of Section 1002 of the Internal Revenue Code.[155] The character of the gain as ordinary or capital is determined by Sections 1245, 1250, and 1231, which provide for depreciation recapture and the possibility of capital gain or ordinary loss. Also, in the case of exchanges, Section 1031 and other provisions of the Code may be applicable where the exchange is wholly or partially tax free. Note that these rules are not specifically applicable when the retirement is by sale at a non-arm's-length price, by contribution of capital to another entity, or through a reorganization.[156]

If the retirement results from an abandonment, loss will be recognized upon retirement. The loss is equal to the adjusted basis of the asset at the time of retirement.[157] If the disposition does not result from an abandonment, the tax treatment will depend upon the characterization of the retirement as normal or abnormal, and upon whether depreciation was based on maximum useful life or on average useful life, since these factors affect basis or affect gains directly.

The second consideration is determination of whether the retirement is normal or abnormal[158] (see *Section 7.3.4* for an analysis of the factors relevant to this distinction). Let us look first at abnormal retirements.

When an asset is retired in an abnormal retirement from a multiple-asset account, gain or loss is to be recognized.[159] The amount of the gain or loss is equal to proceeds less adjusted basis, and adjusted basis is original basis less accumulated depreciation.[160] However, determining accumulated depreciation presents some difficulties because the asset had been part of a multiple-asset account without its own reserve. To recompute the reserve for the asset, depreciation is computed at the rate that would have been proper if the asset had been in an item account; and the same depreciation method actually used for the account is used for the asset.[161] The depreciation rate is based on the average useful life, if that has been used for the account, or on maximum expected useful life if used for the account.[162] Generally, depreciation will be based on average useful life. Note that in these computations no consideration is given to the estimated salvage value for the account, in contrast to the treatment of normal retirements.

The tax consequences of a normal retirement of an asset from a multiple-asset account depends on whether the depreciation had been based on its average expected useful life or on the maximum expected useful life of all assets in the account.[163] Where average useful life of the asset has been employed, the full cost or other unadjusted basis of the retired asset is removed from the account. This identical amount is then subtracted from the reserve. However, a negative reserve cannot be created[164] (see *Section 7.3.5*). The amount of estimated salvage value (after the optional salvage value reduction, equal to 10 percent of unadjusted basis, where applicable)[165] that was set up for the asset then becomes the adjusted basis of the asset for the purposes of computing gain or loss.[166] Thus, gain or loss is measured by the difference between actual salvage proceeds and estimated salvage value. A gain results when actual proceeds are lower.

When the estimated salvage value amount is set up as the adjusted basis of the asset, it appears that the adjusted basis of the remainder of the account is to be reduced accordingly, although the Regulations do not so specify. This adjustment is probably made through the reserve account rather than the asset balance; at least this inference can be gleaned through a comparable salvage value adjustment under the Class Life ADR System. Table 18, in which a $3,000 asset with a $500 salvage value is retired in an ordinary retirement, illustrates the basis adjustment described in this paragraph. The two adjustments described can be combined into one step. The basis of the retired asset for determining gain or loss is $500.

When an asset is retired from a multiple-asset account, and depreciation had been based on the maximum expected useful life of the longest-lived asset in the account, a different tax accounting treatment applies. The amount that would constitute accumulated depreciation if the asset had been in an item account must be computed.[167] This accumulated depreciation amount is determined at the rate that would have been proper if the asset had been in a single asset account; that is, the depreciation method must be the same as the method actually used, and the rate must be based upon the maximum expected useful life determined for the account.[168] This accumulated

TABLE 18

	Basis	Reserve	Salvage	Depreciable Balance
Account before asset retirement	$10,000	$6,000	$1,000	$3,000
Asset retirement	(3,000)	(3,000)	—	—
Salvage value adjustment	—	500	(500)	—
Account after asset retirement	$ 7,000	$3,500	$ 500	$3,000

depreciation amount is then deducted from the unadjusted basis of the asset. The balance is the adjusted basis for determining gain or loss.[169] Note that this method is similar to the treatment of abnormal retirements and that estimated salvage value is consequently ignored.

When an asset is retired through a transfer to a supplies or scrap account, but is not disposed of, a special rule applies to the treatment of gain or loss. First, gain will not be recognized.[170] Loss will be recognized only if a set of complex requirements, discussed in subsequent paragraphs and *Section 7.3.7,* are met.[171]

There are no actual proceeds when an asset is transferred to a supplies or scrap account, but there is a "deemed proceeds" amount in such a situation. The deemed proceeds are the higher of estimated salvage value or the fair market value of the asset at the time of retirement. Loss is equal to adjusted basis of the asset less the deemed proceeds amount.[172] This loss will be recognized only if the retirement is one of three types: (1) abnormal retirement,[173] (2) normal retirement from a single asset account,[174] or (3) normal retirement from a multiple-asset account, but only if the depreciation rate was based on the maximum expected life of the longest-lived asset contained in the account.[175]

The types of retirement (normal versus abnormal) are described in *Section 7.3.4.* The use of maximum life is described in *Section 7.3.3.* Special mandatory grouping rules in conjunction with normal retirements from a single-asset account are described in *Section 7.3.7.*

7.3.7 Special Mandatory Grouping Rules

When an asset is transferred to a supplies or scrap account as part of a normal retirement from a single-asset (item) account, loss will be recognized.[176] On the other hand, if the taxpayer used multiple-asset accounts, these retirements would not generate recognized losses. Consequently, there is an incentive for using single-item accounts.[177] To offset this incentive, the regulations provide for mandatory groupings of item accounts into multiple-asset accounts in certain situations, to prevent distortion of income.[178]

Some tax authorities have taken the position that the mandatory grouping rule is not limited to retirements into a supplies or scrap account, but applies to all retirement under the more complex alternative rules of *Section 7.3.6,* or even to all retirements when Class Life ADR depreciation is not elected. Consequently, the reader should be on notice that interpretations contrary to those expressed by the author have received some significant degree of acceptance.

The number of assets and the similarity of useful life are factors that determine whether the use of item accounts results in a distortion of income. Four situations are listed in order of their potential for distortion:

1. Where the taxpayer has few depreciable assets and these assets have a narrow range of lives, the use of item accounts and the recognition of losses on retirement will generally not distort income.[179] This lack of distortion exists because maximum life does not differ greatly from average life.[180]

2. Where the taxpayer has only a few depreciable assets and chooses to account for them in single-asset accounts, the allowance of losses may possibly distort income when the assets cover a wide range of lives, since average life is substantially different from maximum life.[181] If the distortion occurs, losses are allowable only to the extent they would be allowable from a multiple-asset account; for example, on termination of the account.[182] This rule is applicable only when the depreciation rate for each account is based on the average useful life of all assets.[183]

3. Where a taxpayer has more than a few depreciable assets, but not a large number of depreciable assets, the use of separate accounts and the allowance of losses on normal retirements may in some situations substantially distort income if the same life is used for each account.[184] In such a situation, the item accounts may be treated as a multiple-asset account.[185]

4. Where the taxpayer has a large number of depreciable assets and depreciation is based on the average useful life of these assets, the allowance of losses on normal retirement of these assets will distort income, according to the Regulations.[186] The distortion here will result whether the assets are similar or dissimilar.[187] Consequently, retirements will be treated as if the assets were accounted for in a multiple-asset account or accounts.[188]

Where the mandatory grouping rules cause losses on normal retirements through transfers to a supplies or scrap account that is not to be recognized, special provisions apply to the treatment of these losses.[189] We must first consider the basis of the asset and the measurement of loss before describing how the loss is to be treated. Where the retirement is made from a multiple-asset account, the full cost of the asset less estimated salvage value is deducted from the reserve.[190] The amount of the estimated salvage value becomes the basis of the asset in the supplies or scrap account.[191] See the example (Table 18) in *Section 7.3.6* for an application of this technique. There, the adjustment to the reserve was made in two steps: The full unadjusted basis was deducted, and salvage value was added back.

If the asset had been accounted for in a separate account, a different rule would apply. The loss then would be measured by the adjusted basis less salvage value. Again, salvage value would be deducted from adjusted basis because the asset had acquired the salvage value as its basis in the supplies or scrap account.

This unrecognized loss might, at the option of the taxpayer, be amortized and recognized through annual deductions from gross income.[192] The loss is taken into account in equal annual amounts.[193] The amortization period is the average expected useful life applicable to the asset at the time of retirement, not the remaining useful life.[194] The Regulations provide this example of amortization of the loss: If an asset is retired after six years of use and at the time of the retirement depreciation was being claimed on the basis of an average expected useful life of ten years, the loss would be amortized over the ten-year period beginning from the time of retirement.[195]

7.4 Retirements Under the Guideline Class Life System

Retirements under the Guideline Class Life System are generally treated in the same manner as retirements under facts-and-circumstances depreciation (see *Sections 7.3.1–7.3.4*). This discussion is concerned only with the differences between the two systems.

A taxpayer who elects to utilize the Guideline Class Life System for one or more guideline classes may regroup assets in a guideline class.[196] The accounts may be regrouped to conform to the asset guideline class, that is, so that each account will include only assets in the same class.[197] The regrouping can be effectuated without permission of the Internal Revenue Service, but it must be used for succeeding taxable years.[198]

A retirement is considered a normal retirement unless the taxpayer shows that the retirement was due to a cause not contemplated when setting the depreciation rate and depreciation life (see *Section 7.3.4*). For the purposes of the Guideline Class Life System, the actual expected useful life, not the class life, is to be used.[199]

In an abnormal retirement, gain or loss is equal to proceeds less adjusted basis.[200] Adjusted basis is the original basis less accumulated depreciation. Accumulated depreciation in turn is based on the depreciation rate and life that would have been employed if the asset had been depreciated in an item account. For this purpose, useful life is the class life, not the individual useful life of the asset.[201] Since the class life depreciation period is generally shorter than the actual useful life, an asset is likely to be more fully depreciated. Consequently, adjusted basis will be less, gain (if any) will be higher, and loss (if any) will be less.

Unlike other items, repairs are treated quite differently under the Guideline Class Life System than under facts-and-circumstances depreciation in that the repair allowance is applicable at the election of the taxpayer.[202] Guideline Class Life assets are combined with Class Life ADR assets by guideline class for purposes of the repair allowance.[203] If the repair allowance is utilized and eligible expenditures exceed the maximum repair allowance, the excess is capitalized in a "special basis vintage account"[204] (see *Section 7.2.6*). At the election of the taxpayer, a portion of this basis is allocated to abnormal retirements of Guideline Class Life property to increase recognized loss or decrease recognized gain.[205]

REFERENCES

1. 11(d)(3)(x).
2. 11(d)(3)(x).
3. 11(d)(3)(i).
4. 11(d)(3)(i).
5. *B. R. Kittridge,* (CA-2)88F.2d 632, 37-1 USTC 9165; *P. Dougherty Co.,* (CA-4) 159 F.2d, 47-1 USTC 9117, cert. den. 331 US 838.
6. *Alexander Bros. Lumber Co.,* 22 BTA 153, Dec. 6700, acq.; *V. R. Williams,* 19 TCM 106, Dec. 24,050(M), TC Memo 1960-19.
7. 11(d)(3)(i).
8. 11(d)(3)(ii).
9. 11(d)(3)(ii)(*a*).
10. 11(d)(3)(ii)(*b*).
11. 11(d)(3)(ii)(*c*).
12. 11(d)(3)(ii)(*a*).
13. Section 1250(c), Section 1245(a)(3), Reg. Sec. 1.1245–3.
14. Reg. Sec. 1.1250–1(d)(5).
15. 11(d)(3)(ii)(*b*).
16. Section 1245(a)(3), Reg. Sec. 1.1245–3.
17. 11(d)(3)(ii)(*b*).
18. 11(d)(3)(ii)(*b*).
19. 11(d)(3)(ii)(*c*).
20. 11(d)(3)(ii)(*c*)(*1*).
21. 11(d)(3)(ii)(*c*)(*1*).
22. 11(d)(3)(ii)(*c*)(*1*).
23. 11(d)(3)(ii)(*c*)(*2*).
24. T.I.R. 1097, August 12, 1971, 717 CCH 8683.
25. 11(d)(3)(ii)(*c*)(*2*), 11(d)(3)(vi).
26. 11(d)(3)(ii)(*c*)(*2*).
27. 11(d)(3)(ii)(*c*).
28. 11(d)(3)(ii)(*c*), Example (1).
29. 11(d)(3)(ii)(*c*), Example (2).
30. 11(d)(3)(iii).
31. 11(d)(3)(iii).
32. 11(d)(3)(iii).
33. 11(d)(3)(iii).
34. 11(d)(3)(ix)(*b*).
35. 11(d)(3)(ix)(*a*).
36. 11(d)(3)(iii).
37. 11(d)(3)(iii).
38. 11(d)(3)(iii).
39. 11(d)(3)(v).
40. 11(d)(3)(iv)(*a*).
41. 11(d)(3)(v).
42. 11(d)(3)(iv)(*a*).
43. 11(d)(3)(iv)(*a*).
44. 11(c)(2)(ii), 11(c)(2)(iii).
45. 11(d)(3)(iv)(*a*).
46. 11(d)(3)(iv)(*a*).
47. 11(d)(3)(iv)(*a*).
48. 11(d)(3)(iv)(*b*), Example (1).
49. 11(d)(3)(iv)(*a*), Section 1245(a)(1).
50. 11(d)(3)(iv)(*b*), Example (2).

51. Section 167(j)(2).
52. 11(d)(3)(v).
53. 11(d)(3)(v).
54. 11(d)(3)(v)(*a*).
55. 11(d)(3)(v)(*e*), Example (1).
56. 11(d)(3)(v)(*e*), Example (2).
57. 11(d)(3)(v)(*b*).
58. 11(d)(3)(v)(*e*), Example (3).
59. 11(d)(3)(v)(*c*).
60. Section 179(d)(2)(A), Section 179(d)(2)(B).
61. 11(d)(3)(v)(*d*)(*1*).
62. 11(d)(3)(v)(*d*)(*2*), Reg. Sec. 1.47–1(e)(4).
63. 11(d)(3)(v)(*d*)(*2*), Reg. Sec. 1.47–1(e)(4).
64. 11(d)(3)(v)(*d*)(*1*).
65. 11(f)(5)(ii).
66. 11(d)(3)(v)(*d*)(*1*).
67. 11(f)(5)(i).
68. 11(d)(3)(v)(*d*)(*1*).
69. 11(d)(3)(v)(*d*)(*1*).
70. 11(d)(3)(v)(*d*)(*1*).
71. 11(f)(5)(i).
72. Rev. Rul. 70–624, 1970–2 CB 55.
73. 11(d)(2).
74. 11(d)(2)(vii)(*a*).
75. 11(d)(3)(vi).
76. 11(d)(3)(ii)(*c*)(*1*).
77. 11(d)(3)(vi).
78. 11(d)(3)(vi).
79. 11(d)(3)(vi).
80. 11(d)(3)(vi).
81. 11(d)(3)(vi).
82. 11(d)(3)(vi).
83. 11(d)(3)(vi), Example.
84. 11(d)(3)(iii).
85. 11(d)(3)(iv)(*a*).
86. 11(d)(3)(iii).
87. 11(d)(3)(vii).
88. 11(d)(3)(vii)(*b*).
89. 11(d)(3)(vii)(*b*).
90. 11(d)(3)(vii)(*d*)(*2*).
91. 11(d)(3)(vii)(*d*)(*1*).
92. 11(d)(3)(viii)(*a*).
93. 11(d)(3)(viii)(*a*).
94. 11(d)(3)(viii)(*c*), 11(d)(3)(viii)(*b*).
95. 11(d)(3)(vii)(*a*).
96. 11(d)(3)(vii)(*c*).
97. 11(d)(3)(vii)(*c*).
98. 11(d)(3)(iii).
99. 11(d)(3)(ix).
100. 11(d)(3)(ix)(*a*).
101. 11(d)(3)(iv)(*a*).
102. 11(d)(3)(ii)(*c*), 11(d)(3)(ii)(*b*).
103. 11(d)(3)(ix)(*a*)(*1*).
104. 11(d)(3)(ix)(*a*).
105. 11(d)(3)(ix)(*a*)(*1*).
106. 11(d)(3)(ix)(*a*)(*2*).
107. 11(d)(3)(ix)(*c*), Example.
108. 11(d)(3)(ix)(*b*).
109. 11(d)(3)(ix)(*b*).
110. 11(d)(3)(ix)(*b*).
111. 11(d)(3)(xi).
112. 11(d)(3)(xi).
113. 11(c)(2)(ii), 11(c)(2)(iii).
114. 8(a).
115. 8(a)(1).
116. 8(a)(2).
117. 8(a)(4).
118. 8(a)(3), 11(d)(3)(i).
119. 7(a).
120. 7(a).
121. Rev. Rul. 66–111, 1966–1 CB 46; Rev. Rul. 68–4, 1968–1 CB 77; Rev. Rul. 70–383, 1970–2 CB 54; *H. Shainberg,* 33 TC 241, Dec. 23,838(Acq.); *Harsh Investment Corp.* (DC)71–1USTC 9183; Rev. Rul. 73–410.
122. 7(a).
123. 7(b).
124. 8(c)(2), 8(a)(3).
125. 8(a).
126. 8(a).
127. 8(c), 8(a)(3).
128. 8(b).
129. 8(b).
130. 8(b).
131. 8(b).
132. 8(b).
133. 8(b).
134. 8(e)(2).
135. 7(b).
136. 7(b).
137. 7(b).
138. Rev. Rul. 69–291, 1969–1 CB 62.
139. 7(b), 8(e)(2).
140. 8(e)(2).
141. 7(b).
142. 7(b).
143. 7(b).
144. 8(a)(1).
145. 8(a)(2).
146. 8(a)(4).
147. 8(a)(4).

148. 8(a)(4).
149. 8(a)(4).
150. *Simmons Mill and Lumber Co., Inc.,* 22 TCM 894, Dec. 26, 213(M), TC Memo 1963–185.
151. *T. O. Campbell,* 32 TCM 451, Dec. 31,953(M), TC Memo 1973–101.
152. *United California Bank,* 41 TC 437, Dec. 26,601; aff'd per curiam, (CA-9) 340 F.2d 320, 65–1 USTC 9202.
153. *W E G Dial Telephone, Inc.,* 25 TCM 133, Dec. 27,856(M), TC Memo 1966–41.
154. *Tanforan Co., Inc.,* (DC) 313 F.Supp 796, 70–1 USTC 9452; aff'd per curiam, (CA-9) 462 F.2d 605, 72-2 USTC 9492.
155. 8(a)(1), 8(a)(2).
156. 8(a)(1), 8(a)(2).
157. 8(a).
158. 8(b).
159. 8(c)(3).
160. 8(c)(3).
161. 8(c)(3).
162. 8(c)(3).
163. 8(c)(1), 8(c)(2).
164. 8(c)(1).
165. Section 167(f).
166. 8(c)(1).
167. 8(c)(2).
168. 8(c)(2).
169. 8(c)(2).
170. 8(a)(3).
171. 8(a)(3).
172. 8(a)(3).
173. 8(a)(3)(i).
174. 8(a)(3)(ii).
175. 8(a)(3)(iii).
176. 8(a)(3)(ii), 8(d)(1).
177. 8(d)(1).
178. 8(d)(1).
179. 8(d)(1).
180. 8(d)(1).
181. 8(d)(1).
182. 8(d)(1).
183. 8(d)(1).
184. 8(d)(3).
185. 8(d)(3).
186. 8(d)(2).
187. 8(d)(2).
188. 8(d)(2).
189. 8(d)(4), 8(e)(1).
190. 8(c)(2).
191. 8(c)(2).
192. 8(d)(4), 8(e)(1).
193. 8(e)(1).
194. 8(e)(1).
195. 8(e)(1).
196. 12(a)(5)(iv).
197. 12(a)(5)(iv).
198. 12(a)(5)(iv).
199. 12(d)(2)(iii), 8(b).
200. 8(c)(3).
201. 12(d)(2)(iii).
202. 11(d)(2).
203. 11(d)(2)(iii).
204. 11(d)(2)(vii), 11(d)(3)(vi).
205. 11(d)(3)(vi).

Form **4832**

Department of the Treasury
Internal Revenue Service

Class Life (ADR) System

▶ Attach this form to your return. ▶ See separate instructions.

1974

Names as shown on return (if consolidated return, indicate name and identifying number of electing company)

Identifying number

NOTE: By filing this form you elect, consent, and agree to apply the provisions of section 1.167(a)–11 of the regulations.

Part I Election Questions

	Yes	No
A. Did you exclude under the special 10 percent used property rule property first placed in service this taxable year?		
B. Did you exclude any other eligible property for which an election was not required or permitted? (See instruction 1)		
C. Did you allocate the unadjusted basis of a special vintage account in this taxable year?		
If Yes, attach a statement showing the computation and allotted basis amount.		

	Yes	No
D. Did you change the depreciation method for any vintage account this taxable year?		
If Yes, attach a statement showing the account and the computation of allowable depreciation under the new method.		
E. Did you elect to compute depreciation on a composite guideline class basis in accordance with Revenue Procedure 64–21 for electric or gas utility property under section 1.167(a)–11(b)(4)(iii)?		
If Yes, attach a statement showing the computation.		
F. Check first-year convention adopted this taxable year: ☐ Half-year ☐ Modified half-year		

Part II Asset Guideline Class Summary (See instruction 2)

a. Asset guideline class	b. Unadjusted basis at end of year	c. Asset depreciation range depreciation this year	d. Reserve for depreciation at end of year (Do not include first-year depreciation)	e. Excess of reserves for section 1245 accounts includable in income under section 1.167(a)–11(d)(3)(ix)	
				(1) Section 1245 gain	(2) Other gain
Totals { ▶ Enter totals from columns b and c on appropriate lines of depreciation schedule of your tax return. ▶ Enter totals from columns e(1) and e(2) on appropriate lines of Form 4797.					

Total additional first-year depreciation from Part III, column c. Enter here and include on additional first-year depreciation line of depreciation schedule in tax return . . . .

120

Part III Depreciation (Furnish the following information by individual accounts for assets placed in service this taxable year)

a. Asset guideline class (See instruction 3)	b. Unadjusted basis		c. Additional first-year depreciation	d. Gross salvage value (before application of section 167(f))	e. Period (years)	f. Method	g. Depreciation for this taxable year
	(1) Amount placed in service first half of this taxable year	(2) Amount placed in service second half of this taxable year					
1							
2							
3							
4							
5							
6							
7							
8							
9							
10							
11							
12							
13							
14							
15							
16							
17							
18							
19							
20							
21							
22							
23							
24							
25							
26							
27							
28							
29							
30							
31							
32							
33							
34							
35							
36							
Totals							

121

Form 4832 (1974)

Page 3

Part IV — Treatment of Repair, Maintenance, Rehabilitation, or Improvement of Property

Complete lines 1–21 only for guideline classes for which you elected repair allowance this taxable year (See instruction 4)

	(A)	(B)	(C)	(D)	(E)	(F)
1 Enter asset guideline class number for each class ▲						
For Repair Allowance Property in Vintage Accounts (lines 2–8)						
2 Unadjusted basis at beginning of this taxable year						
3 Unadjusted basis at end of this taxable year						
4 Total (Add lines 2 and 3)						
5 Ordinary retirements in prior taxable years multiplied by 2						
6 Balance (line 4 less line 5)						
7 Ordinary retirements this taxable year						
8 Balance (line 6 less line 7)						
For Other Repair Allowance Property (lines 9–11)						
9 Unadjusted basis at beginning of this taxable year						
10 Unadjusted basis at end of this taxable year						
11 Balance (Add lines 9 and 10)						
12 Total (Add lines 8 and 11)						
13 Average (line 12 divided by 2)						
14 Repair allowance percentage (See Revenue Procedure 72–10)						
15 Maximum repair allowance (line 13 multiplied by line 14)						
16 Excluded capitalized additions (Do not include on lines 17 or 18, Attach schedule describing nature.)						
Repair, Maintenance, Rehabilitation, and Improvement Expenditures for this Taxable Year						
17 Expenditures identified by asset guideline class						
18 Expenditures permitted under Regs. sec. 1.167(a)–11(d)(2)(v)(a) to be indirectly allocated by asset guideline class						
19 Total repair, maintenance, rehabilitation, and improvement expenditures (Add lines 17 and 18)						
20 Deductible repair allowance (line 19—not to exceed line 15)						
21 Capitalized property improvements (line 19 less line 20)						

Complete lines 22 and 23 for asset guideline classes for which you do not elect the repair allowance this taxable year (See instruction 4)

22 Repair expense for repair allowance property . . . . $

23 Capitalized amount for repair allowance property . . . . $

Part V — Asset Retirements (See instruction 5)

a. Asset guideline class	b. Original unadjusted basis of asset guideline class	c. Unadjusted basis of assets retired during this taxable year	d. Unadjusted basis of assets retired in prior taxable years	e. Gross salvage value (original estimate)	f. Proceeds
Assets Placed in Service During 1971					
Totals for 1971					
Assets Placed in Service During 1972					
Totals for 1972					
Assets Placed in Service During 1973					
Totals for 1973					
Assets Placed in Service During 1974					
Totals for 1974					

☆ U.S. GOVERNMENT PRINTING OFFICE : 1974—O—548—159   52—0781521

123

Index

Acknowledgments

A number of sessions on Class Life ADR depreciation recently sponsored by the American Management Associations have been a valuable source of ideas, techniques, and strategies for the use of that system of depreciation. Those sessions, of which I was pleased to serve as chairman, were held in New York and Chicago. The following speakers deserve special mention:

John O. Hatab, Manager, Price Waterhouse & Co., New York.
Karl Ruhe, head of the Office of Industrial Economics, U.S. Treasury.
Raymond F. Gehen, Valuation Specialist, Coopers & Lybrand.
Lana Feinschreiber, attorney in New York City.
Hilton L. Sokol, Manager, Oppenheim, Appel, Dixon & Co.
Oded Aboodi, Partner, Arthur Young & Co., New York.
C. J. Smith, Jr., Assistant Treasurer, Dow Jones & Co., Inc., Princeton, N.J.
James T. Lyon, Assistant Vice President, Taxes, Chessie System, Baltimore.
David A. Kelly, Manager, Arthur Andersen & Co., Chicago.
Stanley J. Gradowski, Manager, Price Waterhouse & Co., Chicago.
Harvey Coustan, Partner, Arthur Young & Co., Chicago.
Robert A. Lamar, Tax Manager, Arthur Young & Co., New York.
Eli H. Fink, Manager, Haskins & Sells, New York.
Donald A. Mulligan, Manager, Arthur Andersen & Co., New York.
Martin J. Linker, Manager, Ernst & Ernst, New York.
Edward Fitzgerald, Manager, Arthur Young & Co., Chicago.
Thomas S. Oehring, Partner, Haskins & Sells, Chicago.
William H. Frewert, Partner, Touche Ross & Co., Chicago.
Robert W. Lynch, Supervisor, Ernst & Ernst, Chicago.
Harold U. Friedman, Principal, Coopers & Lybrand

Without the efforts of four men, this book would not be possible. Emil Sunley, now Director of the Office of Tax Analysis of the U.S. Treasury, and Ernest Christian, now U.S. Tax Legislative Counsel, were instrumental in the development of the Class Life ADR depreciation system. Edwin S. Cohen, then Assistant Secretary of the Treasury for Tax Policy, and John S. Nolan, then Deputy Assistant Secretary of the Treasury for Tax Policy, provided the impetus.

My interest in tax depreciation began a decade ago when I was teaching at Yale with Ralph C. Jones, John Burton, and William Bruns. Among my own teachers, special thanks are due Boris Bittker, Marvin A. Chirelstein, and George Lefcoe at Yale Law School; Gerald Brady and Russell Taussig at Columbia Graduate School of Business; and the Graduate Tax Faculty of New York University Law School.

Contact with the following people proved beneficial: IRS engineer agent Jake D. Dow; revenue agent Frank Rochefort; Stephen Weltman, Howard Koff, and Phil Dalziel, all formerly of Chrysler Corporation; and Howard Miller and Richard Karl Goeltz of Joseph E. Seagram & Sons, Inc.

Special mention should also be made of the many fine BNA portfolios on depreciation written by James T. Lyon.

Additionally, a number of persons at the American Management Associations have been instrumental in the development of this book, including Pat Daly, John Metralexis, Robert Rachlin, and Tom Gannon.

Thanks are also due Marilyn K. Bartle, who was able to read my handwriting well enough to type the book.

D